RAISING POSITIVE
LITTLE PEOPLE

BEING AN AWESOME PARENT USING LOVE, NOT DISCIPLINE, BY CREATING BOUNDARIES AND LISTENING TO YOUR CHILD

HOLLY HENDERSON

HOLLY & HIVE PTY LTD

CONTENTS

Behind every child who believes in himself, is a parent who believed in them first.

Matthew L. Jacobsen

INTRODUCTION

Being a disciplinarian is no fun. Nobody likes to be the big, bad, rule enforcer who hates fun and is constantly saying no—but sometimes it feels like that's the only option. When your children won't listen to you, you have to resort to extreme forms of discipline if you're going to get anywhere. Right?

Wrong.

Chances are, sometimes you feel like the only interactions you have with your child are negative. You may scream, yell, constantly correct, or feel like you are dishing out a new punishment daily. These negative interactions may even leave you thinking you're missing out on so much with your child because they have created a sense of disconnect.

The worst part is that no matter how much you try to correct your child's behavior, nothing seems to work. You take away things, ground them, or give them more chores, but to no avail. You fear that despite all your efforts, there is no hope. You know that something needs to change before you completely lose the loving connection you once had with your child, but you're not sure how to make that change.

If you are using traditional disciplinary methods, you are unlikely to see an improvement in your child's behaviors or in your relationship with them. Yes, you might be using the same methods as parents before you to deal with a tantruming toddler or a rebellious teenager, but research shows that there's a better way. You want to make the most of every minute with your child, not lose precious time to conflicts and frustration.

This book will teach you how to discipline with love and compassion while still getting effective results. This approach covers all the necessary parts of discipline while cutting out the harmful and maladaptive ones. You'll discover why certain tactics, like positive reinforcement, work, while others, like spanking, don't—and be able to better apply them as a result.

With the strategies you'll develop, you'll find yourself handling conflict like a pro. This book isn't about keeping children happy 24/7, but instead is about treating them with understanding and creating a healthy family environment. You'll develop a deeper connection with your child as you learn to see things from their perspective while still maintaining your role as a parent. At the end of the day, you'll find you're a better parent than you were yesterday.

You will feel confident in your ability to discipline your child in a healthy and constructive way. You will learn how to encourage positive behaviors while at the same time teaching your child essential skills they will continue to develop and strengthen throughout their life. Finally, you will understand that the best solution to improve your child's behaviors and your relationship is to regularly reflect on both you and your child's emotions and behavior. If you are ready to become the parent you've always wanted to be, let's get started by addressing the foundation upon which your parenting approach is built.

1

CREATING A SOLID FOUNDATION

D iscipline is an essential, but often frustrating, part of being a parent. Whether you're establishing disciplinary expectations for the first time or looking to change your current approach with your children, it can often feel like you have no idea where to start. In this chapter we're going to take a look at the essential groundwork you must do before you can discipline effectively. This involves understanding the goal of discipline and assessing your current relationships and family dynamics.

The Role of Discipline

Discipline is something that becomes a part of our everyday lives starting at a young age. Adults are expected to use discipline when making daily choices such as getting out of bed to go to work versus hitting snooze and going in late. We also adhere to certain rules and laws to avoid disciplinary actions, like driving the speed limit to avoid receiving a speeding ticket. As a parent, though, we find ourselves in the position of instituting and enforcing discipline, as opposed to being on the receiving end. This can feel like new and uncomfortable territory for many parents.

Everyone has a unique experience with discipline that often shapes the way we apply discipline as a parent. Not all parents recognize how their past disciplinary experience interferes with their current perspective and influences their reaction to their child's behavior. To better understand the purpose and effects of discipline, let's begin by discussing what it truly is.

Effective Discipline

Discipline's primary purpose is to foster appropriate behavior so our kids grow up to be emotionally mature adults. Children who learn how to apply self-discipline grow into adults who can:

- Resist instant gratification

- Be considerate of others' needs

- Be appropriately assertive, as opposed to completely passive or inappropriately aggressive

- Exhibit the willpower to do what needs to be done, even when it's inconvenient or difficult

Discipline should focus on teaching children how to self-regulate and remain in control of their emotions. It should also be used to encourage appropriate reactions to strong emotions and tough situations. Effective discipline keeps our children safe while also giving them an opportunity to learn how to take responsibility and make good decisions. To use discipline effectively, it should:

- Be provided by trusted adults who have a strong emotional connection with the child

- Be consistent and directly relate to the behavior that needs to be changed

- Be fair to the child

- Be appropriate to the child's developmental stage

- Be self-enhancing, or result in behaviors that create self-discipline

Discipline should strive to *teach* children how to self-regulate and how to consider the consequences of their actions, both good and bad. It should not focus on forcing children to conform to unfair or unjust rules. Although discipline is a method used to teach children how to follow rules, we want children to understand the connection between their behaviors and the related consequences—whether good or bad.

Discipline is only effective when it is provided in a respectful manner. Both the parent and the child must show mutual respect. While the child must understand authority figures, they also need to feel that their rights and feelings are being considered and not taken away.

Discipline becomes less effective when it is not applied consistently. This is often the biggest struggle for parents. Failing to implement consequences for undesirable behavior every time the child acts up leads to additional confrontation. Children learn when they can get away with poor behavior and when they cannot. They will often push their parents' limits until the parent caves in, because inconsistency leads the child to believe that eventually they will get what they want.

Another issue with inconsistency pops up when caregivers or various adults in the child's life are not on the same page with their expectations. For example, if grandma lets her little darlings eat ice cream before bed each time they stay over or allows them to watch television shows that she knows mom or dad would not approve of, the children may learn that behaviors or rules expected at home don't apply outside the home. As a child grows, this can lead to poor decision-making because they believe that they can "get away" with certain behaviors when their parents or primary caregivers are not present.

Key Relationships

Every family will have its own dynamics and key people who help shape a child. Your family may not include all the relationships described below, and that is okay. However, it is important that you understand and work with the people in your own unique family structure to build strong and healthy relationships. The more aligned everyone in the family unit is, the easier it will be to model appropriate behaviors, avoid confusing your child, and create a strong family structure that provides support to everyone.

With Your Partner

The relationship between you and your significant other will change when you become parents. These changes will likely be positive in some ways, and negative in others. Tension may arise if you and your partner have different parenting styles. One of you may be more authoritarian, while the other may align more closely with positive parenting techniques. Despite these differences in how you each approach parenting, you should be on the same page about setting developmentally-appropriate rules and expectations for your child. You should also make it a priority to maintain a healthy and supportive relationship with your partner, as this plays an integral role in your parenting approach.

Parents may find themselves giving their child all their attention, energy, and time, which can cause their relationship with their partner to suffer. If this occurs, the way you or your partner interacts with your child can then change and can even cause a healthy relationship to turn unhealthy over time. A healthy relationship is one where both people share a common goal for what they want from the relationship and where they want the relationship to go. Other characteristics of a healthy relationship include:

- You and your partner share an emotional connection. You both feel loved, accepted, valued, and respected in the relationship.

- You and your partner feel comfortable disagreeing without fearing retaliation for sharing what bothers you. This means when disagreements arise, neither of you feels humiliated, shamed, or that your feelings are disregarded because the other person needs to be right.

- You and your partner both have lives outside your relationship. You encourage each other to maintain friendships and individually participate in activities that you enjoy.

- You and your partner strive for open and honest communication, which is essential for a healthy relationship. Each of you should feel as though you can express your needs, fears, and desires freely. Communication should also consist of problem-solving together and being able to jointly make big decisions that you both are comfortable with.

Keeping these factors in mind will help you and your partner stay connected. Additionally, you can take extra steps to ensure that the relationship with your partner gets the attention it needs by trying the following:

- Make quality face-to-face time a daily occurrence. Even if it is just for 15 minutes, take that time to give your partner your full attention.

- Schedule regular date nights.

- Do something new together.

- Focus on enjoying your time together and having fun.

- Set aside time to discuss your upcoming week and address concerns or problems that should be resolved.

- Keep the intimacy from fizzling out.

With Your Child

Parents want to have a loving and respectful relationship with their child. Many of us tell our children regularly that we love them, but how often do we ensure that we are making it a priority to create a loving connection with our children?

While there is no one-size-fits-all approach when it comes to creating a strong and healthy connection with your child, most positive parent-child relationships have similarities, such as:

- Interactions between the parent and the child are warm, loving, and encouraging.

- The parents provide plenty of structure throughout the day. Children know what is expected of them, and both the parent and the children establish boundaries. The child is also aware of the consequences for not following household or family rules.

- Parents are empathetic and available to help their child when they encounter problems. However, in healthy relationships, the parents do not immediately step in to solve the problem for the child. Instead, they encourage their child to come up with solutions and try out different approaches to teach the child how to solve problems on their own. The parents are available to provide encouragement, support, and understanding when things may not go as the child expected.

Many parents question their relationship with their child. They will often wonder what they could be doing better. If you are struggling with your child, you too may be constantly asking what you could be doing differently.

The only way you will know where your relationship with your child stands is to ask them. The following questions will help you recognize what areas of your relationship need work and what parts are thriving. When you ask these questions, allow them to come out naturally. Having your child sit and answer all of these questions directly in one sitting might not be the best approach. Instead, ask these questions in a casual manner when the timing is right.

- In what ways do I show you that I love you?

- What do you think I can improve on to be a better mom/dad?

- Do we spend enough time together? How often do we spend quality time together?

- Do you think I give out more compliments or criticism?

- Do I give out fair discipline?

- Do you trust me with everything?

- Do I break promises to you often? Which ones have I not followed through on?

- Do you think you and your brother(s)/sister(s) are treated the same?

- What is one thing you wish I wouldn't do?

- What is something you want me to continue to do?

- What is the one thing you want the most from me?

- What is something I could say to you more often?

If you have multiple children, it is best to ask them these questions separately. They could be influenced by each other's answers, and you might not get an honest response as a result.

Creating Healthy Connections

Pay attention to what goes on between you and your child. This means trying to see things from your child's perspective. There may be times when your child appears to be pushing your buttons or has certain behaviors that you are not enthusiastic about. Remember to remain present with your child and welcome them into your loving arms even in moments of frustration. Creating a healthy connection with your child will not always be easy. If you remain present, you will find that even in the most difficult situation, giving positive attention will allow your relationship with your child to become stronger. It won't drain you, but will fill you with energy.

Remember, establishing a bond with your child is the first step toward creating a life-long connection. Newborns who develop a bond with their parents in the first few weeks of life are more likely to maintain a strong and healthy relationship with their parents throughout their life. If you feel like you have neglected this crucial aspect of parenting, remember that it is never too late to start.

A strong parent-child relationship, just as with any relationship, will take effort. But remember, you'll feel and notice the difference in how you approach parenting and your child when you take the time to make this effort.

Some tips to create healthy connections with your child include:

- Tell your child every day that you love them, no matter what age they are and no matter how difficult the day may have been.

- Spend time playing together. This is often easier with younger children, but as our kids grow we still need to set time aside to do activities with them that they enjoy.

- Dedicate at least 10 minutes a day to talking with your child without distraction. This is valuable time that gives your child an opportunity to open up about things they may be struggling with or to share exciting things going on with them.

- Strong connections require empathy and active listening. This means we allow our children to talk freely without judgment or criticism. As your child talks to you, remember to put yourself in their shoes to better understand their point of view.

- Dedicate quality time to spend with each child. Set aside special times or days that allow you to strengthen your bond with your child and reassure them that they are valued and loved.

Building a positive relationship with your child is achievable for everyone. If you remain present, spend quality time with your child, and create an environment built on trust, respect, and love, your relationship with your child will grow into a healthy and strong connection for the rest of your child's life.

With Your Family Members

Your child will interact with many adults, some of whom will play a vital role in helping them develop into independent and successful adults. Family members such as grandparents, aunts, uncles, and cousins are often important figures in a young child's life. While these family members generally try to do their best, they can at times—often unintentionally—undermine your parenting approach. This can create conflict and strain in your relationship and may also negatively affect the relationship they have with your child. It is not easy to confront certain family members when they are ignoring your wishes.

I can't tell you how many families have a grandparent, aunt, or uncle who lets the visiting children get away with much more than their parents would allow. I often hear grandparents joke with their grandchildren "what happens at grandma's house, stays at grandma's house." This can be frustrating for parents, as it seems to be an obvious disregard for the rules and expectations you have for your children. This also unintentionally can teach children that they don't always have to abide by the rules their parents establish, especially if their parents don't know that the rules are being broken. This, of course, is not the type of relationship you are trying to achieve with your child.

It is not easy to bring up different opinions about parenting with your family members, but it's important to ensure you are all on the same page when it comes to the rules your child is expected to follow and the appropriate disciplinary techniques for enforcing those rules. In order to effectively establish rules and responsibilities for all the family members who may help care for your child, you'll want to keep a few key points in mind.

Be Optimistic

We may naturally feel as though other family members are intentionally showing us disrespect when they bluntly go against the expectations we've established for how our children should be cared for. However, most of the time other family members are acting with the best intentions and trying to offer help or support when they see an opportunity to do so. Not everyone may be aware of the boundaries they are crossing when they try to take a more active role in your child's life. They often are looking for ways to be included and you can easily help them feel needed without being defensive. Before jumping to conclusions and assuming the worst, give your family members the benefit of the doubt, as chances are good that they're trying as best they know how and may just need a little education about your expectations.

Speak up When Someone Crosses the Line

When someone has crossed the line and made you uncomfortable, you are within your rights to politely but firmly speak up. For instance, if your mother is constantly giving you parenting advice that you haven't asked for or insists on caring for your child the way she wants instead of following the way you do things, you can let her know. Simply say that you appreciate the advice and will be sure to ask for help when you need it. Or, you could respond to a family member who inadvertently undermines your expectations for your child by saying that you understand they took a different approach to parenting than yours, but it would be greatly appreciated if rules and consequences are the same from one environment to another to help teach your child that expectations are consistent no matter who may be taking care of them.

When someone crosses the line, you do not want to criticize them or judge their way of doing things. Instead, take this as an opportunity to teach and encourage them to consider the benefits of your approach. Help them understand why you are doing things a certain way and encourage them to ask questions. If necessary, discuss how you can come to a mutual agreement where you both feel supported and respected.

Be Supportive

It is not uncommon for parents to find themselves split between siding with their own parents or supporting their partner. You and your partner both agreed to the parenting approach you are taking with your children, and sometimes this means you will need to establish clear boundaries with your own parents. This can be an uncomfortable position to be in, but you are raising your children with your partner, not your parents. There may be times where you will need to be more direct when sharing your expectations with your parents, but this can be done in a respectful manner. It is important for family members to know that you and your partner are on the same page and that you both support the parenting style you've chosen to use with your children, even (and especially) when that is different from the way one or both of you were raised.

It makes sense that having a strong foundation is key to effective discipline. When your family dynamic is strong, children feel supported and heard. The more you can encourage strong family dynamics not just within your immediate family, but within your extended family as well, the more your child will benefit.

Parental Action Plan

Assess your current relationships with your child, partner, and extended family by answering the following questions:

- Based on the information in this chapter, what are some things you can do to improve your relationships?
- Reflect on how you were raised. What worked, and what didn't? What did you like and dislike about your childhood?
- What things are you carrying over from your childhood to your current parenting approach?

2

TRADITIONAL DISCIPLINE AND REACTIVE PARENTING

Picture this scenario—you are at the kitchen sink washing the dishes when you notice it is abnormally quiet. You call your child's name, but there is no response. You dry your hands and, slightly panicked, begin searching for your child. They aren't watching television or coloring at the dining room table. They have to be in their room or the bathroom. Then you hear little clinks and clanks coming from your bedroom. You open the door to find that an explosion of all your best makeup and nail polish has decorated your formerly neat and well-kept bedroom. You grab your child's arm and begin yelling at them for making a mess, spitting out phrases like "Do you know how much this cost?" or "Do you know how long it is going to take me to clean this!?" or "Why can't you keep your hands off my stuff?" or perhaps "Go sit in time-out until I tell you to come out!"

Maybe you have had a similar experience with glitter being tossed around the room with abandon or markers used to decorate all the walls. You may have had a comparable outburst when you noticed your child was doing something or getting into something they know they aren't supposed to, and you reacted out of frustration. Have you ever said or done things in a heated moment that you later came to regret? If so, you've experienced reactive parenting.

What Is Reactive Parenting?

Under reactive parenting, we react to our child's behaviors based on our emotions. We don't take an objective view of the situation to assess what is the best response. This results in parents exploding out of frustration or desperation. Being reactive is one of the greatest obstacles to parents' ability to remain in control and connect positively with their child.

Of all the challenges you will face as a parent, learning not to be reactive will be one of the hardest. Trying to remain in control of yourself and create a positive connection with your child when they are acting inappropriately is no easy task. Rest assured, nearly all parents struggle with avoiding reactive parenting. Being reactive every once in a while is not generally cause for concern. Rather, the problem arises when reactive parenting becomes the dominant parenting style and makes up a majority of the interaction you have with your child. This means that most of the interaction you have with your child revolves around irritation, anger, or aggression.

"Stop running!"

"Don't do that again."

"Why aren't you doing what I told you to do?"

"Why aren't you ready yet?"

These phrases are common examples of reactive parenting, especially when accompanied by a scornful tone and aggressive body language. We obviously need to correct certain behaviors more sternly when they cause a safety concern. However, in many situations parents find themselves reverting to an aggressive tone while shouting commands at their child. How you view your child's behaviors will significantly affect how you respond to those behaviors. For instance, if you look at your child's behavior as manipulative or done on purpose just to get under your skin, you will more than likely respond to their behavior with more negativity and sternness.

Aside from how you view your child's behaviors, there are a few reasons why you may default to reactive parenting.

You Are Overwhelmed

Stress, lack of sleep, and anxiety are the most common reasons we feel overwhelmed and let our emotions get the best of us. Parents of infants and younger toddlers are prone to not getting enough sleep, making them more susceptible to reactive parenting. But, even if you have slightly older kids, other issues may be keeping you up at night. Balancing work, household chores, bills, and personal relationships while also raising a child is a lot to juggle. These often add up to excess stress and anxiety, which costs us even more sleep. Unfortunately, our kids may get the short end of the stick when it comes to our patience and being able to assess situations with a clear mind.

It is important to remain objective when encountering behavioral struggles with your child. You may be quick to point out inappropriate behaviors and criticize your child for not listening to you when you start to make demands. Remember, when you are deprived of sleep and have other concerns going through your thoughts, the root of your anger in these situations often has nothing to do with your child's behaviors.

You Have Neglected Your Basic Needs

Most parents recognize when they are overreacting to certain situations or become quick to anger when interacting with their child. However, despite recognizing these frustrations, many of us forget to pause and ask what else could be fueling our emotions. HALTing before you continue to address behavioral issues or other conflict with your children is an effective strategy you can use at any point. HALT stands for hunger, anger, loneliness, and tiredness. Checking in with yourself and what other needs you may be neglecting will generally allow you to identify the root cause of your emotional response. Labeling these needs and then satisfying them will allow you to reapproach your child in a calm and clearheaded manner.

Get into the habit of HALTing before interactions with your child. When you wake up, HALT. After work, HALT. Before bed, HALT. Regularly checking in with yourself will allow you to be more present and positive with your child.

You Reinforce Behaviors Learned From Your Own Parental Figures

At one point you were in your child's shoes and it is not uncommon for many parents to mimic the way their parents raised them, whether they support the parenting style of their parents or not. Some parents will use the way they were raised as a guide for what not to do with their kids, while others will use their upbringing as the template for how they raise their kids. Regardless, many of us are unaware that our views about how we were raised influence the way we approach our own children.

Take a moment to look back to how your parents used discipline with you. What type of parenting style did they typically exhibit? What feelings did they invoke in you that you may be trying to protect your child from experiencing? How might you be overcompensating to ensure your child knows that they are loved in a way that your parents may not have shown you?

Remember, the relationship you build with your child is the first of many relationships they will experience. Having a strong and healthy relationship with your child will provide them with a positive example of how their future relationships should work.

The Issue with Reactive Parenting

There are many ways reactive parenting can hurt the relationship you create with your child. It also gives your child the wrong impression of how a relationship should work. A child who is exposed to reactive parenting more often than responsive or positive parenting will develop misguided ideas around relationships. They may think that being abusive (verbally, physically, or emotionally) is normal and will begin to treat others in this manner.

Reactive parenting also teaches your child that, when you are frustrated or angry, it is okay to be hurtful or to criticize others. Children model their parents' behaviors, and so if you are constantly reacting to your child's behaviors with anger and frustration, that is how they will begin to react to others when they are mad or frustrated.

Traditional forms of punishment are often still thought of as the most effective way to discipline a child. How often were you spanked or put into time-out as a child when you acted out of line? While many parents may not fully agree with these types of corrective measures, they still utilize them when disciplining their child because of their own experiences.

Traditional punishment has a negative impact on the relationship you have with your child. These types of punishment often emphasize obedience, as opposed to focusing on teaching a child how to better respond in certain situations. There are a few reasons why reactive parenting should be avoided, which include:

- Traditional forms of punishment are often unleashed in moments of frustration or high emotions. This is not a teaching strategy, but instead resembles an adult version of a temper tantrum. For example, if your child acts up while shopping because you won't buy them a chocolate bar or toy, what is your most common reaction? Do you grit your teeth, make threats, or state how they will be punished when they get home? While you may not be yelling, crying, or whining, this attitude is not far off from how your child is reacting to being told no to what they want. The main difference is that you have all the power. When you throw an adult tantrum, you expect your child to willingly bend to your request and be easy to control. Your child has the same expectation, but has no power to get you to bend to their will.

When we lapse into reactive parenting, we are unconsciously telling our child that any time we feel tired, stressed, or distracted, we may unleash fury onto our children regardless of their behavior or intentions. This gives a child conflicting feedback. Multiple studies show that children who are disciplined using aggressive punishments are more likely to be aggressive themselves. They may struggle more with mental health issues and are more likely to exhibit antisocial behaviors later in life.

What makes spanking, hitting, or other physical punishments even more damaging is that they often continue to gradually become more physical. Parents who feel that this type of punishment is the only way to get their children to comply will often keep escalating the punishment. What begins as a light smack on the hand to remind a child to keep their hands off things that don't belong to them can escalate into using objects like a belt or a wooden spoon to spank a child when they misbehave. While physical punishment might halt some behaviors temporarily, it is often ineffective at correcting behaviors in the long term. Instead, more inappropriate and rebellious behavior is likely to occur as the child continues to grow. Reactive parenting often teaches children inappropriate ways to control their own emotions and is more likely to reinforce undesirable behaviors.

- Reactive parenting does not allow room for compassion or understanding. Our emotions are too influenced by other factors. Many times we are not actually reacting to what our child is doing, but instead we are reacting to another factor like being tired, hungry, or stressed. Many times our response to our children's behaviors has nothing to do with what they have done; they unfortunately are just caught in the crossfire of what we are feeling. With reactive parenting, there is no pause to consider what other factors could be driving these emotions. Since your child remains unaware of why you are so upset, they will often think that they are inherently bad or will feel guilty for making you so upset.

- Reactive parenting may not always come off as overly aggressive. Many parents will 'cave' to a child's tantrums or demands because they simply cannot keep fighting and repeating themselves. To give an example, let's look at 'Debra.' She is exhausted from a long day at work when she picks her son up from school and heads home. In the car, her son asks to play video games when they get home. Debra says no because he needs to do schoolwork first and also reminds him of a book project he needs to finish. Once home, Debra quickly changes her clothes, throws in a load of laundry, and washes a sinkful of dishes she was too tired to get to the day before. While she is doing all this, her son is still asking for his video games. Debra continues to repeat herself and ask him to start his homework, but finally caves in when he asks for what seems like the 100th time just as she notices that dinner is burning in the oven. She screams at him, "Fine, just go do whatever you want since you aren't going to listen to me anyways!" She slams the oven door and feels even more frustrated and defeated. The rest of the interactions between Debra and her son that evening are filled with anger. She barks demands at him and at one point snatches his game controller out of his hand and throws it in a box, forbidding him to play video games for a week. There are several other negative comments Debra spits out at her son, and once the day is done she deeply regrets all the negativity that filled their evening.

Most of us can probably empathize hearing that Debra reacts with such frustration when her son continues to ask for something she has already told him 'no' to. Many parents have found themselves in similar situations, where they just reach a breaking point. After they finally give in to their child, they are usually filled with frustration and instead of addressing the real issue, they allow this frustration to dictate the rest of their interactions with their child that day. The entire time, the child is unaware of the underlying reason why their parents are feeling so frustrated and angry.

The Antidote to Reactivity

Being a responsive parent is the opposite of reactive parenting. With responsive parenting, you focus on understanding what your child's behavior is trying to communicate and then provide them with effective strategies to self-regulate their emotions.

Responsive parenting requires parents to practice mindfulness. This means we remain calm and make the choice not to react to our feelings when we experience negativity towards our child's behaviors. We acknowledge that we are angry, but we pause before responding.

Responsive parenting allows you to evaluate your child's behaviors with more clarity. What, in the moment, may appear to be manipulative or disrespectful may actually be your child formulating effective strategies. While these strategies may not be appropriate, they may eventually lead to key skills your child will need later in life. You don't want to discourage your child from strengthening these skills, but you do need to formulate appropriate strategies for your child.

For instance, 'Abby' and 'Sam' had a happy and relentless six-year-old named 'Lisa.' They, like many parents, labeled her "picky eater." They admitted that she was not so much picky as just refusing to eat what they put in front of her. At first, the behavior was limited to dinner time. She would refuse to eat what her parents had made and an hour or two later, once everything had been cleared away, she would begin to whine about being hungry.

Not wanting to feel as though they were depriving Lisa of the basic need for food, they would make her whatever she requested—usually a peanut butter and jelly sandwich or a bowl of cereal. However, now dinner became a huge battle. Lisa refused to even sit at the table, complaining that she didn't like what was made, even if it was a meal that had previously been one of her favorites. Additionally, the behavior started to include lunchtime and even breakfast.

Abby and Sam tried reasoning with her, bribing her, and even resorted to making Lisa sit at the table by herself until she ate something from her plate. If Lisa took just one biet, her parents would then make her what she wanted. But, Abby and Sam became fed up with the behavior. They yelled and fought with Lisa daily about her eating habits until they were at a loss. They didn't want Lisa to starve, but they also knew Lisa was taking advantage of them to get the food she wanted instead of what she needed. Lisa would throw a fit at the table on a nightly basis and in the morning it would start all over again.

Your child has probably done something similar as well. Every meal, there is a new reason why they don't like what is on their plate. They don't like green foods, the mashed potatoes are touching the corn, the carrots are too round... This is your child assessing the situation. They know what they want and they are looking for the most effective ways to get out of eating what is in front of them.

While this seems manipulative, your child is actually beginning to make use of their strategy skills. They are testing out what works, and often will subtly make you aware of it. Has your child ever commented, while you are making dinner, that they don't like what you are making or asked if their favorite snack was available? This is your child's subtle way of letting you know they don't want to eat what you are cooking, and they have formulated a strategy of their own to get what they want. These are skills you will eventually want to encourage in your child, as knowing how to be appropriately strategic is essential in life, but for mealtime, it is easy to see how this can come off as manipulative.

After discussing a plan of action, Abby and Sam established new expectations for mealtimes. Lisa needed to eat what was served but could then have a small, after-meal treat. Her options for the treat were a piece of fruit, some yogurt, or occasionally a piece of candy or ice cream. If she refused to eat, she would be allowed to have a few plain crackers to hold her over until breakfast, but nothing else. When they sat down for dinner after clearly explaining the new expectations, Lisa immediately complained that she didn't like what was served for dinner and pushed her plate away. Abby and Sam held their ground and reiterated that Lisa had to eat what was on her plate, or her only other option until breakfast was a few crackers. The first few dinners were unpleasant for Abby and Sam. Lisa threw her food on the floor, cried, and pleaded for something to eat. She crumbled the crackers and threw tantrums like Abby and Sam had never seen before. But Abby and Sam held firm. Abby even allowed Lisa to participate in choosing what was for dinner and reminded Lisa about the expectations for eating what was served. Lisa sat down and ate peacefully with her parents that evening. She was rewarded with two small after-dinner cookies. Eventually, every night was pleasant and peaceful. While they still have a few instances where Lisa refuses to eat, she accepts that if she doesn't eat, she gets some crackers and will have to wait until the morning for breakfast. There are no huge blowups or tantrums, because Lisa understands the expectations.

Now, you may be rolling your eyes or even doubting your ability to follow through on setting new limitations with your child. You know how uncomfortable and frustrating it can be to hear your child screaming when they are struggling to adapt to new limitations. In the moment, it will be hard, but remember, you can address undesirable behaviors calmly and responsively now, or you can deal with even more problematic behaviors and greater struggles later. It does require patience to implement responsive parenting techniques, but you and your child will benefit greatly in the long run.

Exercises to Help Stop Reactive Parenting

If you are a reactive parent or have reactive parenting moments, this doesn't mean you are a bad parent. Everyone has moments where they become overwhelmed and let their emotions get the best of them. There are a few things you can do for yourself and your child to defuse the situation and allow you to remain in control when facing challenges.

Self-Care

If you are not taking care of yourself, you will struggle to properly take care of those around you. Many parents, especially moms, avoid self-care practices because they think it makes them selfish or takes time away from caring for their children. However, self-care is not just about bubble baths or pampering yourself. Self-care means providing yourself with the same love and attention you give to others. Taking time to ensure that your needs are being met will lower the risk of suffering from burnout and will help you remain in control of your emotions and reactions.

Self-care can also help you combat unnecessary stress. Parents who are stressed are more likely to lose control of their emotions. This is why it can be helpful to choose some self-care activities that also help reduce stress.

Self-care is essential to help you maintain good mental health, and it can also be used as a way to show your children that they need to make taking care of themselves a priority. You don't have to shower yourself with gifts or even clear away an hour every day; instead, focus on spending just 10 minutes every day doing something that you enjoy, and do it for yourself. Read a book, listen to music, color a picture, or set some bigger goals and dedicate time to work on the steps to achieve them.

Each parent should have a little time to themselves during the week. Work together to schedule a time when you each can have a break. Once a week, one parent should take over the parental duties completely (for example, take the kids for a walk or get them out of the house for a short while). The other parent gets to use this time to relax and rest. This benefits both parents, as one parent has the opportunity to connect with and spend a little extra quality time with the children while the other parent can get in some much-needed self-care.

Counted Breathing

Addressing your child's behavior when you are struggling with your own emotions is a recipe for frustration. It is important that you recognize when your emotions are getting the best of you and combat them with effective calming techniques. One of the best things you can do, no matter where you are or the situation you are facing, is counting to 10 or higher. As you count, focus on keeping your breath under control. You can temporarily excuse yourself from the situation to give yourself a break and count your breaths away from your child. Giving yourself some space will help you gain control of your emotions so you can approach your child with more consideration and understanding.

Identify Your Triggers

Reactive parents will often have specific triggers that initiate explosive reactions. To take control over your emotions, you need to evaluate what causes you to overreact to your child's behaviors. If you are a reactive parent, it is likely that your parents were also reactive parents. This can be a good starting point in understanding your own behaviors. Also, consider what happens throughout your day that may contribute to responding negatively to your child's behaviors. Do you notice you are more on edge after a stressful day at work, and on those days you are less patient or understanding of your child? How do you take care of yourself? Do you notice you are more short-tempered on days when you don't exercise, or when you eat a lot of snacks and processed foods?

There are many internal and external factors that can cause you to default to reactive parenting. It is important to uncover your triggers and then honestly evaluate how those triggers relate to your child's behaviors. Identify the behaviors you know are likely to cause you to react negatively. Once you know which behaviors are more likely to set you off, you can create a plan to prepare ahead of time. How can you approach these behaviors with more compassion and understanding? Remember, be a role model for your child and react how you would expect your child to react.

What Are Your Child's Triggers and Needs?

Recognizing what triggers your child to behave in certain ways will help you identify what your child really needs from you when they misbehave. When your child is hungry, tired, or bored, they are more likely to exhibit undesirable behaviors. Many young children are unable to express what it is they need; this unfortunately can make it harder to pinpoint the cause of your child's stress. Begin to look for patterns with your child's behaviors. Do they tend to be more rambunctious at a certain time of the day? Do certain activities cause them to misbehave? Transitions or changes in your regular routine can also cause some children to become anxious and overwhelmed. Tune in to what else is going on that could be triggering your child's behaviors and then come up with a few ways you can try to avoid any meltdowns or tantrums you anticipate might occur.

Also remember that we all have bad days and we all make mistakes. As an adult, you probably wish for a little compassion on your bad days; extend some compassion to your kids on their bad days, too.

Focus on Connection First, Then Correction

Children, just like adults, need to feel heard and loved. It is vital that you place an emphasis on connecting with your child no matter what the situation is. Reinforce that you hear them and you are aware that they are struggling with some big emotions. Being emotionally in tune with your child will help keep the situation from escalating.

You don't have to agree with your child, but you can acknowledge their emotions and hear what they are saying. Use reflective language and body language to connect with your child. For instance, if they are mad you can mirror their expression by frowning too. Then say to them, "You seem very angry. Is there something I can help you with?" It is hard not to jump right into enforcing disciplinary measures to correct the misbehavior, but a more effective way to do this is by connecting first and correcting second.

By showing your child you understand what they are feeling, you will maintain a strong connection with them. When conflicts come up in the future, they will be more easily resolved.

While it may be clear to you now that traditional discipline does more harm than good, many people unknowingly buy into common myths about discipline that can actively damage the parent-child relationship. Let's dive into what those myths are and discover the truth about them.

Parental Action Plan

Recall a recent interaction with your child where you responded out of frustration. Assess the situation from a new perspective and ask yourself: Did I embody reactive parenting at that moment? If so, what could I do differently next time?

If you keep a journal, consider adding a section that details the situations when your child misbehaved or cried. Have another section that lets you track the times you reacted to your child's behaviors out of anger. By recording these interactions, you'll be better equipped to notice patterns or triggers to your child's behavior and your own responses.

3

DEBUNKING DISCIPLINE MYTHS AND MISCONCEPTIONS

Discipline is often associated with punishment, but the truth is that these are two very separate tactics. While discipline can include punishment, the most effective parenting approaches exclude punishment from their toolbox. Understanding common misconceptions around discipline will lead to embracing new, more positive disciplinary techniques.

Myth: Discipline and Punishment Are the Same

Fact: Both discipline and punishment enforce following the rules. However, one teaches children how to observe and correct their misbehaviors for the long term while the other relies on negativity to stop a behavior in the current moment.

Punishment is a negative form of discipline that is used to immediately stop behaviors. The idea is that when the child is unhappy due to the punishment, they will quickly stop doing what is frustrating their parents. Punishment usually involves one of the following:

- A reactive approach that stops the behaviors in the moment

- Making a child 'pay' for their mistakes

- Parental reactions that are often fueled by frustration or desperation

- Focuses on controlling your child, not teaching them how to control themselves

Punishment has more to do with making a child "suffer the consequences," with an emphasis on suffering when the child breaks rules or misbehaves. Parents will yell, spank, take away privileges, call names, or embarrass their child as a type of punishment. All of these approaches begin to wear down a child's confidence and establish the false belief in the child that they are simply a bad person. While punishment will often get a child to stop what they are doing, it is rarely effective at correcting behaviors in the long term. Instead, punishment often leads to:

- Punishment creates confusion for the child in terms of what behaviors are not appropriate for them but can be used by their parents. For instance, when Dominic hits his little brother for taking his toy, Dominic gets spanked and his toy is given to his brother. Why is it okay for mom or dad to spank Dominic for doing something wrong, but he is not allowed to do the same to his brother when his brother did something wrong?

- Punishment does not teach a child to control themselves. Instead, the child expects their parents to control them and never learns to regulate their own behaviors.

- The child does not learn how to peacefully or appropriately resolve problems. They also are not taught that their behaviors can turn a small problem into a much bigger one.

- Certain punishments, like being forced to sit in the corner for long periods of time, only give the child time to become more frustrated at how unfair the punishment is. Most children will spend their time-outs justifying their actions, which results in resentment and distance between the child and parent. Some children will enact some form of revenge on their parents, such as giving the silent treatment or being cold towards their parents.

Discipline uses techniques that remind a child that their behaviors have consequences, but these consequences can be positive or negative. Positive discipline focuses on discouraging undesirable behaviors while teaching children to make a different choice when faced with a similar situation in the future.

Positive discipline handles behaviors in one of the following ways:

- Shows the child the connection between what they do and what happens next (cause and effect)

- Proactively handles the situation by teaching useful skills for the future

Discipline is about teaching the child new skills or strategies to solve their own problems and remain in control of their emotions. Consequences imposed through discipline have clear time limits, where with punishments the consequences last until the parent arbitrarily decides they're over. The benefits of discipline include:

- Relies on a proactive approach to behaviors instead of a reactive approach

- Encourages children to learn from their mistakes

- Maintains a positive parent-child relationship

- Reduces attention-seeking behaviors

- Strengthens the child's confidence and their ability to manage their own emotions and behaviors

Many disciplinary methods focus on positive reinforcement. Parents may establish a reward system or give out praise when they notice their child exhibiting positive behaviors.

Myth: Discipline Is Not Effective Because Parents Are Too Easy on Their Kids

Fact: The main reason why discipline fails is because it needs to be used consistently.

Discipline should not focus on getting a child to obey the commands of the parents. If you use discipline simply to get your child to do what you want, you are not teaching your child the skills they will need to navigate life as an adult. Using discipline in an appropriate manner leads to children who grow into emotionally mature adults; this requires consistency.

If expectations are not predictable or reliable, children will naturally become confused. This results in more frustration during future conflicts and parents begin to feel resentful. A prime example of this is the "do as I say, not as I do" approach some parents take with discipline. When children are faced with this type of dissonance (meaning that your actions do not align with your words), they receive mixed messages about what is expected of them.

Discipline becomes ineffective and will take much longer to produce positive results when parents are inconsistent with disciplinary actions. When you warn your child about a consequence for continuously misbehaving, you need to ensure that consequence is something you can and will follow through on.

To implement discipline effectively, be clear about the goals you are trying to accomplish. For instance, you can have a reward chart that encourages a child to use their manners, share with their siblings, clean their room, or help with other household chores. The goal for the reward chart is first to teach your child the appropriate behaviors or expectations. Then, once they have been prompted enough times to understand what behaviors are expected, they are rewarded for using these behaviors on their own. The child learns that this behavior—such as saying please and thank you—is expected of them. The reward chart can be used to work towards a bigger reward, such as a trip to their favorite ice cream shop or to the playground, after they have demonstrated they understand how to consistently use their new good behaviors.

Myth: Punishment and Yelling Are the Only Ways to Make My Child Listen to Me

Fact: Punishment is ineffective for changing long-term behaviors or enforcing rules. Children who are yelled at are more prone to anxiety and depression.

Verbal discipline like yelling can have a long-lasting negative impact on your child. Consider how you feel when you are yelled at. How would you react if your boss started yelling at you because of a minor mistake on a report you emailed that took less than two seconds to correct? Would you feel embarrassed, confused, or hurt? This is no different than how a child feels when they are yelled at. Are you more likely to do what someone demands of you when they yell at you to do it? For most, that's a no, and again, this is the same when a child is yelled at.

Yelling is demeaning, but it is a default reaction that many parents revert to out of anger. For the most part, yelling is a reaction to things parents wish they could change about their child. We wish that, when we say it is time to put shoes on and go because we are running late, our child would dutifully stop what they are doing and immediately put their shoes on. We wish our teens would pick up their phone to call us when there's a change in plans and they are going to be somewhere else, or when they are running 10 minutes late. Some repetitive behaviors that seem, to the parents, to be easy to correct may often result in parents having an outburst and yelling.

It is crucial that you remain calm and collected when addressing behaviors you wish your child would change. If you are one of the parents who believes yelling and screaming is the only way to make your child listen, let's take a look at some of the reasons why yelling does not work.

Triggers Fight-or-Flight Mode

Yelling appears effective because it scares your child. This may suddenly shock your child into stopping what they are doing because they are pushed into fight-or-flight mode. Everyone has this physiological reaction to fear. If the brain perceives something in our environment as a threat, it shifts into fight-or-flight mode as a survival mechanism, and certain areas of the brain shut down.

In a child, the learning center of their brain is temporarily switched to the off mode when their fight-or-flight response is triggered. That means it is not possible for a child to learn or retain information when they are in flight-or-flight mode. When you yell at your child, their brain starts to perceive you as a threat. Their brain then turns off their learning system in order to boost activity in the part of the brain that is responsible for keeping them protected.

Speaking calmly and respectfully to your child keeps their learning center active. This also reassures your child that they are safe, which makes them more receptive and understanding of the lessons they need to learn to change their behaviors in the future.

Devalues Your Child

The fastest way to make your child feel devalued is resorting to yelling. Constantly being subjected to this type of verbal punishment diminishes a child's self-worth and makes them doubt their capabilities. Yelling makes your child feel like they are your enemy. You never want to make your child feel like you are against them, so you need to react to your child in a way that does not make them feel "less than" who they are. Using a calm tone lets your child know that they are loved and, despite the mistake they may have made, they are still valued and worthy of your love and respect.

Causes Anxiety, Depression, and Lower Self-Esteem

Children who are regularly yelled at are more likely to suffer from anxiety, depression, and lower self-esteem. When parents use harsh verbal discipline—such as screaming, insults, or cursing—they are causing their child to experience frequent episodes of anxiety. Being yelled at is not a soothing experience and even if you are loving and soothing to your child during all of your other interactions, yelling can still negatively impact your child's mental well-being.

Studies have shown that yelling at a child has similar negative effects to using physical punishment (Wang, 2013). Children who are disciplined using harsh verbal commands will typically struggle with their behaviors across many settings. They often have more behavioral problems than they should, do not do as well academically as their peers, and exhibit significantly more delinquent behaviors. Using yelling as a form of discipline can cause setbacks in your child's brain development.

Creates Disconnection

When we yell, there is no display of empathy, which is essential for supporting a strong bond with your child. Yelling implies that you are not on the same side as your child and it puts you at odds with them. When a child no longer feels their parents support them or understand them because they are constantly being yelled at, there is almost always going to be an increase in poor behaviors. Yelling can lead to a child being more defiant and defensive. They lose trust in you and will no longer feel safe with you or free to talk openly with you. When you yell at your child, you are creating a disconnect with them. No child that is yelled at will feel closer to their parents as a result of the yelling. Instead, children will feel more disconnected, alone, and disappointed.

Leads to Poor Communication

Children already have a hard time regulating their own emotions, and it is your responsibility as the parent to teach your child how to cope with big emotions. If a parent continually yells at a child when the child is upset, this is only teaching the child to handle their anger in the same way. Yelling activates the mirror neurons in a child's brain. When you yell, your child is more than likely going to feel an urge to yell back. The good news is that the mirror neurons work the same way when you react to your child with respect and peace, promoting a similar response from your child.

Myth: Spanking Is an Effective Form of Discipline

Fact: Spanking causes adverse effects on the parent-child relationship and hinders a child's overall development.

Physical discipline, like spanking, is used by parents to try to improve a child's behaviors. It is thought that if a child endures physical pain, they will associate this pain with the behaviors they need to change. However, you cannot spank the behaviors out of your child. Various studies have found that spanking is not only ineffective at correcting a child's behaviors, but it actually often causes behaviors to become worse (Heilmann et al., 2021). Though hitting your child may temporarily cause them to stop a specific behavior, it does not help correct these behaviors in the long term. Your child will simply stop a behavior because they are afraid of getting hit, not because they know it is wrong or understand what appropriate behaviors they should be using instead. While discouraging undesirable and socially unacceptable behaviors is not a flawed intention, using a method like spanking to discourage these behaviors is flawed.

The negative consequences of spanking include:

- Children who are spanked will become more aggressive. They are also more likely to resort to using physical force to resolve conflicts.

- Children who are spanked suffer from alteration in their brain development, which increases antisocial behaviors. Areas of the brain that are supposed to help regulate emotions and detect threats overreact to emotional responses, even those that are non-threatening. Children may withdraw from peers as their brain learns to register a connection with others as a threat.

- The child develops disruptive behaviors in school or outside of the home.

- Children who are hit are more likely to be diagnosed with oppositional defiant disorder (ODD). This is characterized by temper tantrums, argumentative behavior, refusal to follow rules, vindictiveness, active defiance, and spitefulness.

- As physical punishment increases in occurrence, the child's behaviors become increasingly worse. It is not uncommon for parents to then escalate physical punishments to get a child to comply, and this leads to the child becoming even more poorly behaved.

- Even parents who typically have a more nurturing or warm parenting style will still see worse behaviors if they resort to physical punishment with their child.

When you feel out of control due to your child's behaviors, give yourself a time-out. Calm yourself down and collect your thoughts so you can address the issue at hand in a respectful and effective manner.

Myth: There Is No Difference in the Types of Disciplinary Approaches

Fact: There are four parenting styles that have been outlined through various research. Each parenting style exhibits different characteristics and typical outcomes.

Every parent has their own unique troubles when it comes to raising their child. No child is the same, so there is not a complete one-size-fits-all technique that works the same with every child. Just as no child is the same, no parent is either. Every parent has their own style and default approach to raising their children. These different parenting styles should have one common theme, though: to raise children so that they will grow into independent, respectful, and mature adults.

There are four parenting styles that parents will often relate to—authoritative parenting, authoritarian parenting, permissive parenting, and neglectful parenting. Key characteristics of each parenting style are defined as follows:

Authoritative

Authoritative parents provide clear expectations for how their child should behave. They also establish consistent consequences for misbehavior. Authoritative parents provide structure, but are affectionate towards their children. They allow for flexibility in their approach because they include their children in problem-solving strategies that will help manage their emotions and overcome challenges they face.

Authoritarian

Authoritarian parents also establish clear expectations and strict consequences for their child's behaviors. However, they are not very affectionate with their children. They also use their parental role as justification for keeping their children at a lower 'level' than they are. Phrases like "because I'm the parent and what I say goes" or "I'm the parent, I make the rules" are regularly used by authoritarian parents.

Permissive

Permissive parents are the opposite of authoritative parents. These parents shower their children with love and affection. They have very few, if any, structured expectations in place to help their child through difficult emotions or situations.

Neglecting

This is considered the least effective type of parenting. As the name suggests, neglectful parents do not show their children affection or provide guidance with regards to discipline for their children. Children of neglectful parents are often left to "fend for themselves" or figure it out on their own.

Studies have shown that children who have authoritative parents exhibit more positive behaviors in home and school settings than children whose parents have another parenting style (Howenstein et al., 2015).

Myth: Children Learn Self-Control by Being Controlled

Fact: Children learn self-control through various experiences. They do not learn when there are too many restrictions placed on them or they are constantly told what to do.

Controlling a child to get them to comply with the demands of their parents is rooted in the notion that children do not want to do what is right on their own. However, children naturally want to do what makes their parents and those around them happy. They rely on their parents and other caregivers to guide them in making the right choices.

Trying to control a child does not teach them self-control; it only limits their opportunities to practice developing their own self-control. Controlling your child is more about forcing the child to be obedient. When you control your child, you deprive them of the experiences that will help them learn essential skills needed to grow into high-functioning adults. Giving your child the opportunity to learn from their experiences, use their problem-solving skills, practice self-calming techniques, and even try out their negotiation skills is the best way for them to develop self-control.

Myth: Obedience Equals Respect

Fact: Obedience can be obtained through mutual respect, but is often inflicted through tactics that create fear (to avoid punishment) or resignation (being forced to do something by controlling caregivers).

An obedient child does not always equate to a respectful child. A child may learn to comply and obey out of fear, not respect. Children who experience harsh punishments learn to listen to adults in the interest of avoiding more punishments. In these situations, obedience is only practiced because the child is complying to the will of the adult out of fear, not out of respect.

Respect comes when the child takes the wants and needs of others into consideration and also understands that their own needs and wants are being considered. Respect will not come from a child giving in to what a parent says or giving up on themselves.

Respect and obedience can arise mutually, but only when both are rooted in love and connection. Children will willingly comply with requests from adults when they are directed to do so in appropriate ways, not through punishment or control.

Forcing a child to obey and do what they are told to do can lead to bigger issues, which is another consideration to keep in mind. If a child is not taught to respectfully say 'no,' or taught that they are allowed to have their own opinions, they will often have a hard time making the right choices or saying no to peers as they grow.

For instance, if you only expect your child to obey you without ever saying no or asking why, you are teaching them (unconsciously or consciously) to obey authority figures without question. This may lead your child to become overly docile to the opinions of other authority figures such as teachers, coaches, bosses, or other adults. If your child is not allowed to stand up for their beliefs or desires at home, then how will you expect them to stand up for their beliefs as an adult?

What about other, more common situations your child will certainly encounter? For example, when your child is a teenager, will you be able to trust that they will have the skills needed to turn down drugs or alcohol if friends offer them? If you are not encouraging your child to voice their own opinions in a respectful manner when they are young, they won't learn to trust their instincts and be able to walk away from situations that lead to poor decision-making. Instead, they will look at the situation as "everyone else is doing it, so I have to do it too."

Questioning the need for obedience is not always appropriate, but you need to teach your child when they can challenge what is being said to them and when they do need to follow the rules that apply to everyone.

Myth: Compromises Makes Me a Weak Parent

Fact: Negotiating with your child can teach them life skills without turning you into a pushover.

Negotiating with your child will help them develop key skills and teach them how to appropriately ask for what they want. Finding a compromise can also teach your child that there are many situations they will encounter that require give and take.

How often have you asked your child to do something like take out the trash and they don't do it, but then they ask you for a ride to their friend's house? Most parents are inclined to respond to their child's request with a flat "No, I asked you to do something and you didn't do it. Now, you can't get what you want." This only teaches the child that they must do what is asked of them immediately because otherwise they will never get the things they want. In this sense, they are only giving.

Instead, this type of situation is the perfect time to demonstrate how compromises can work. You can remind your child that you asked them to take out the trash, but they did not do it. Now they want something from you. You could say to them, "Something does not seem right about this situation," and ask them what they think can be done to fix it.

You do not have to give in to your child's every request. There are many times where compromises cannot be made, and your child needs to learn to accept and cope with these situations as well. Allowing your child to exercise their right to respectfully take part in decision-making, when appropriate, is crucial for your child to learn about boundaries. This is also the best way to teach them how to tune into their own feelings and recognize when something doesn't feel right. While you want your children to make sound decisions, you also need to give them the opportunity to disagree and then help create a plan that is suitable for both parent and child.

Now that we've dispelled these common myths, let's take a look at some reasonable expectations to have for your child. Obviously there is no "one-size-fits-all" approach, but distinct ages require different techniques in order to be developmentally appropriate.

Parental Action Plan

Think of times you punished your child for the same thing over and over again (or if you are a new parent, times as a child when you were repeatedly punished for a specific behavior).

Were those punishments effective?

What was the actual outcome? Did it create distance or connection between you and your child?

4

WHY DO THEY DO THAT? DEVELOPMENTAL EXPECTATIONS

I t makes sense that children require different disciplinary tactics at different ages. After all, as they get older and begin to understand more about the world around them, it becomes easier to explain the need for rules and structure. But this doesn't always mean that things get easier with age. In this chapter, we'll look at appropriate expectations for different ages and what tends to motivate misbehavior at each age.

Developmental Considerations

Your child's stage of development should provide you with an understanding of appropriate expectations for your child. Their developmental progress is essential for implementing effective discipline strategies. If you try to force your child to do too much, too soon, you and your child will be frustrated, disappointed, and set up to fail.

Infant: Birth to 12 Months

No discipline is necessary and infants should be encouraged to explore the world around them and see where their curiosity takes them. However, boundaries should be established and things they should not be getting into should be eliminated from their environment as much as possible.

Infants need to become accustomed to schedules for feeding, sleeping, and socializing. When your child begins to move, you can start to teach them things that are off-limits or unsafe. If your crawling baby is making their way towards something that is dangerous, calmly tell them 'no.' Then remove them from the situation or provide them with a more appropriate activity.

Babies are far too young to comprehend cause and effect. Therefore, trying to set consequences for their behaviors will only hinder their development. At this stage, you will be teaching your baby to trust you by providing them with their daily needs. This is also the ideal time to strengthen your bond with your baby through frequent one-on-one play time.

Parents often think their infants can do far more than they may be developmentally capable of. While it may seem they are trying to provoke you or manipulate you with their crying, they are simply learning how to communicate their needs and wants.

Early Toddler: One to Two Years of Age

Toddlers begin to experiment with their control of their surroundings. They are attempting to exercise their own will, as opposed to that of others.

It is essential that parents understand and have a high tolerance for their child's curiosity and learning. Encouraging growth and independence is essential for proper development at this stage.

Late Toddler: Two to Three Years of Age

Late toddlers are learning how to express themselves and are gaining vital skills at this stage. This can cause more frequent episodes of frustration as they begin to recognize their limitations. Children at this age rarely try to misbehave on purpose.

Parents should be empathetic towards their children's frustration while also setting safe limits for their children.

Preschool and Kindergarten: Three to Five Years of Age

Most children at this age have a better understanding that their actions have consequences. They are beginning to learn what behaviors are appropriate and what behaviors are not. However, children are not fully developed at this age and will often struggle to demonstrate good judgment.

Children at this age are more receptive to verbal rules and visual cues. Your goal is to communicate household rules in a clear and simple manner.

When it comes to their behaviors, you need to establish expectations ahead of time and have them reiterate the expectations to show they understand.

Punishing behaviors that are not first explained will make it hard for your child to understand what they are being punished for. By this age, they are able to comprehend that there are rules they need to follow and when they deviate from these rules, they have to accept the consequences for their choices.

Time-outs are effective at this age, when enforced properly. When sitting in time-out, your child should not have access to toys or electronics. Sending them to their room, for this reason, will not be sensible. Decide on a consistent time-out spot; a step or chair placed away from distraction are the most common time-out zones. When your child is in time-out, avoid giving them any attention, such as talking or eye contact. Giving them this attention reinforces undesirable behavior. Use a timer to establish when the time-out is over. As a general rule, time-outs should be kept to one minute per year of age (for example, a four-year-old will sit in time-out for four minutes). Once the time-out is over, communicate with your child about why they were told to sit for a few minutes. For instance, if you asked them to clean up a mess and they refused, you would explain to them that we need to clean up after ourselves because it is unfair to expect others to clean up after us all the time. You should also calmly discuss what your child could do next time to better handle the situation that got them into a time-out. If they were put in time-out because they were not following directions and doing what you asked, such as cleaning up their building blocks from the kitchen table, be sure they follow through with those directions once the time-out is over. Also, end on a positive note by giving your child some form of affection, like a hug.

Remember, discipline is about encouraging good behaviors. This has just as much to do with praising good behaviors as it does with setting consequences for misbehavior. The more you focus on the desired behaviors, the more likely your child is to repeat them. What you give attention to is what your child will do more of.

Children at the preschool to kindergarten age need direct instructions. Telling your child not to run in the house does not help them figure out what to do instead. Rather, remind your child to walk in the house. Also avoid phrasing your directions as a question. Saying to your child, "Will you come sit down at the table for dinner?" gives the impression that 'no' is a legitimate response. Instead, be clear and say, "It is time for dinner, and you need to come sit at the table." Instructions need to clearly state what your child should do and eliminate any question as to whether or not they need to follow the instruction.

School Age: 6 to 12 Years of Age

Children in this age range are starting to want more independence, which can lead to conflict. This is also the age when parents tend to make unrealistic threats, which in turn discredits whatever consequences have been established. At this age, your child is going to quickly pick up on and remember when you do not follow through with a consequence. They may also become more aware of your limits and how far they can push until you give in to their request.

It can also be tempting to implement more severe punishments for repeated offenses or serious misbehaviors. However, taking away privileges for long periods of time can actually discourage a child from changing their behavior. If you take away everything, they have nothing else to lose so they aren't as concerned about what consequences may arise. While taking privileges away can be effective, there needs to be motivation for your child to make better choices. Create goals for your child to reach so that they can earn their privileges back through good choices.

Preteens, or children between 9 and 12, learn best from natural consequences. While natural consequences can be applied to any age group, children at this age are now mature enough to cope with the consequences of their choices and behaviors. If you are constantly telling your child to put their shoes by the door when they come home from school but you usually end up helping them search the house to figure out where they left their shoes when they want to go out to play, you can allow natural consequences to reinforce better behaviors. You can remind your child to put their shoes where they need to be, but be clear that if they do not put their shoes away, you will not be helping search for them. When your child wants to go out to play and cannot find their shoes, they experience the natural consequence of losing time playing because they are wasting it looking for their shoes.

Another common situation parents encounter is fighting with their children to complete their homework. Many parents will allow their children to stay up late to get it done, or some parents may even give extra help with the homework so their child gets it done faster. However, staying up late and missing sleep will often lead to more struggles the next day, whether that's difficulty getting your child up for school or having the child make poor choices due to exhaustion. Instead, if their homework does not get done before their standard bedtime, your child must go to school without completing it. They will then have to deal with the natural consequence, which is often a poor grade or having extra homework to complete the next day.

Most parents do everything in their power to ensure their child is successful in all they do. However, kids need to learn from their mistakes, and this means you need to let your child fail sometimes. When you allow your child to experience the natural consequences from their poor choices, they are more likely to self-correct and properly assess the positive and negative consequences of their actions.

For some children, certain natural consequences do not seem to work. For example, if they get a failing grade for incomplete homework it is no big deal to them, even if it means extra work during the summer. If this is the case, your child may need a little extra reinforcement from you. Implementing a rule that homework must be done before they are allowed to use electronics is one example of a way you can use natural consequences in a slightly modified manner.

Adolescents: 13 to 18 Years of Age

Peer groups begin to influence kids' behaviors during this age range. Kids will begin to distance themselves from their parents, challenge family dynamics, and face internal and external conflicts around who they are and what they want to become.

While children of this age appear to want more freedom to figure things out on their own (which they should be encouraged to do, to an extent) they still need parental guidance. Even though children may not show it, they are still looking to their parents for support and approval. It is vital for you to remain present in your kids' lives, especially in times of conflict.

At this age you have already laid the foundation for your children to make suitable choices and understand the consequences of their actions. Discipline is still necessary for teens; they need to understand what is expected of them in new and changing situations. New rules will need to be created. For example, if your teen is driving, there need to be clear rules about when they should be home and when they are allowed to use the car, among other things.

Teenagers want control, so giving them more independence can reduce conflict and maintain respect. Allow them to make their own choices about certain things, like what after-school activities they want to participate in. You can expand these choices when they consistently exhibit positive behaviors.

During the teenage years, you still want to focus on positive behaviors and praise your child for making good choices. Remember to reward this positive behavior, as opposed to only punishing poor behavior all the time. For example, if your teen consistently fails to be home by curfew, you might be tempted to revoke their driving privileges for a week and also change their curfew to an earlier time. However, moving up their curfew is an extra layer of punishment. Instead, establish what behaviors are necessary for your teen to gradually earn a later curfew.

Also remember that by this age, your child has developed empathy and can better understand your perspective and put themselves in your shoes. Explaining to them why you are frustrated or upset can be an effective way to get them on your side and connect with them. This is a far better approach than coming off as a cold disciplinarian who is perpetually angry with them.

Now that we've laid the groundwork for effective, respectful discipline, it's time to jump into the practical stuff. Over the next few chapters, we'll explore various methods of discipline that aim to resolve common disciplinary issues and encourage healthy relationships.

Parental Action Plan

Considering the age of your child, have your expectations for them been too high or too low?

Review the expectations you have established for your child, and ask yourself if your child is at an age where they can comprehend those rules and consequences. Consider revising the rules and limitations in place to better suit your child's developmental needs. Also, think about how the new set of rules can further encourage their development.

5

BUILD BETTER BOUNDARIES

M any parents know that it is important to establish consistent boundaries with their children. But what does it really mean to set boundaries, and what do healthy ones look like? Learning how to set and communicate practical, effective boundaries helps your child understand and adhere to them.

What Are Boundaries?

When you think of boundaries, what often comes to mind first? Are there rules for your children to follow? Do you have expectations for their behavior both at home and outside of the home? Although all of this contributes to establishing boundaries, it's important to note that boundaries are not just a set of rules. Boundaries are how you define your role as a parent to your child. They create a healthy relationship between you and your child that is built around respect, love, and values. Ultimately, boundaries help you, as a parent, remain loving and supportive to your child but still maintain your separate identity as an adult.

Children push boundaries in many ways. Your school-age child may interrupt you while you are having a conversation with another adult or may join in on the conversation without being invited into it. Your toddler may tell you what you are going to do today and then throw a tantrum when the day does not involve a trip to the playground, ice cream shop, or toy store. Your child may disregard your privacy and barge into your bedroom without your knowledge.

Boundaries, to a child, are often another way for them to test how far they can push you. However, parents also have a tendency to cross boundary lines and it is important to recognize when you may be guilty of this.

Over-Functioning for Your Child

Parents want to see their children succeed in all things, which often causes them to feel anxious about their children. This anxiety may come out as over-functioning, or feeling the need to do too much for your child, which crosses boundary lines. If you are nervous about your child making the right choices or resolving conflict on their own, you may try to take control and provide extra help to relieve your anxiety, even if you have not been asked for help.

When you do more than you should for your child, it is often hard to recognize at first. In many cases, you are just trying to make things easier for your child, but your actions are fueled by your anxiousness. Some common signs you may be over-functioning for your child include:

- You know that what you are doing for your children is something they can do for themselves.

- You ask your child a lot of questions in an interrogative way.

- Your children are always your central focus.

- You over-share your life with your child in the way that you would with a friend.

- Your child often controls the household.

- You live vicariously through your child.

- You have a hard time regulating your own emotions and reactions when you know your child is upset or disappointed.

Over-functioning does not allow your child to figure things out on their own. It eliminates their experience with failure and hinders their potential to learn. While it is painful to watch your child struggle, you need to take a step back and, when appropriate, allow them to handle the situation themselves. You can still provide empathy to your child when they are going through an emotionally difficult ordeal, but you need to let them experience hard feelings and trust that they will bounce back.

Over-Empathizing With Your Child

When we over-empathize, we are typically projecting our own feelings onto our child. This is another situation where anxiety fuels your actions. For example, you may worry that your child will be left out by their peers and therefore allow them to break the rules to fit in. You over-empathize because you do not think your child can handle their own emotions.

Why Boundaries Are Important

Boundaries help you create a secure, safe, and stable environment for your child to grow. However, many parents give their children too much flexibility when it comes to setting and reinforcing boundaries. While you want to ensure that your child is heard and validated, there need to be clear lines drawn that teach them patience, self-awareness, and independence. Too many parents lose their own identity as they raise their children because there are no boundaries to teach the child that their parent has other roles and interests, too.

Setting boundaries is essential for your child's emotional development.

Boundaries Make Your Child Feel Safe

Kids feel insecure without clear limits, and this increases their anxiety. Boundaries give structure to many things throughout the child's day. Meal times, screen time, chores they need to complete, homework times—these are all predictable if clear boundaries are in place.

If you set rules and routines but then allow your child to constantly negotiate changes, it depletes the child's sense of security. If they can talk you into letting them have an extra hour of screen time day after day, the structure of their day becomes unpredictable. Until your child is developmentally advanced, they are not capable of fully grasping why rules are in place and the appropriate times when these rules can be changed. This does not usually happen until your child reaches adolescence.

Establish your non-negotiable boundaries early, and enforce them consistently. You can work together with your child on less important boundaries to encourage their decision-making skills, such as what sport they want to play. However, there are some areas where you, as the parent, know what is best. These are referred to as life-enhancing boundaries, which we will discuss further a little later in this chapter. By establishing some non-negotiable boundaries at an early age, you provide your child with structure. Without these boundaries, a child feels more uncertainty; conflict can result because the child feels unsure of the rules and routines they are expected to follow.

Boundaries Teach Your Child to Connect to the Real World

Young children naturally have a tendency to be narcissistic; this is developmentally appropriate, until a certain age. If a child is taught that their emotions, desires, and needs always come first and control their parents' lives too, they will believe that the world revolves around them. The child then grows into an adult who is narcissistic and has a strong sense of entitlement.

Your child needs to learn that they cannot expect to get their way all the time. Boundaries help children cope with this disappointment and teach them to have patience. They also expose children to struggles that will help them master new skills.

A child who recognizes boundaries can better relate to the world around them. They understand there are certain limitations in place and build up resilience by learning to handle disappointment when they don't get their way. Experiencing disappointment will also help your child be more empathetic, because they will be able to relate to how others feel when they are disappointed. If you are constantly giving your child what they want so they avoid disappointment, they are going to face many challenges as an adult when they are going to be expected to do things for themselves and abide by established rules in various settings like the workplace.

Boundaries Help Minimize Conflict

When there are clear boundaries in place, your child learns that there is no use trying to negotiate those limits. The more consistent you are with reinforcing the boundaries, the less arguing and resistance you will encounter from your child. Your child will learn to expect these rules. This does not mean there will not be occasional negotiating, but you need to keep boundaries firmly in place. Being flexible about when boundaries are expected to be followed (or not) will encourage your child to try to get their way more often because you have, in the past, given them what they want.

Unclear boundaries also confuse children because they are unable to predict how you will react to their behaviors. For instance, parents who work from home need to establish clear boundaries for when they need to work without interruption and when they can give their full attention to their child. If you allow your child to interrupt a work call one day but the next day you become frustrated when they do the same thing, your child becomes unsure of when they can ask for your help and when they need to wait patiently for assistance. Conflict and arguing frequently arise due to this uncertainty.

Establishing Limits and Boundaries

Each family will establish its own unique boundaries, which should meet the needs of both parents and children. No two families will have the same values, boundaries, or expectations, no matter how many parts of the family dynamic are similar. Your family's boundaries should reflect who you are, what you value, and what you believe in. They should reinforce your guiding principles. Boundaries can fall into two main categories when it comes to parenting.

Empowering Boundaries

These boundaries are fair and justified in some way. Empowering boundaries can be clearly explained to children so they understand what is expected of them. Children are more likely to adhere to these types of boundaries.

These boundaries are created in the child's best interests and they often do not participate in establishing these types of boundaries. Habit-forming boundaries are a prime example of empowering boundaries. These provide children with life skills, allow them to feel safe, and help them grow into well-rounded adults. For example, basic habit-forming boundaries might include proper hygiene (brush teeth, bathe, wear clean clothes, wash their hands after using the restroom) and going to school.

Other empowering boundaries may relate to social interactions or be-haviors. These boundaries need to be established so your child learns to be kind, considerate, and respectful. For example, you might set boundaries that they may not use curse words when they talk or bully others.

Keep in mind that for you to set an empowering boundary, you yourself must adhere to this boundary too. For instance, you set a habit-forming boundary that your child cannot have television an hour before their bed-time because they need to get a good night's sleep. You should then also cut off your own screen time an hour before your bedtime. If you want the best results, you can't just tell your child what they need to do to be healthy and happy; you have to model it and show them.

Parent-Ego Boundaries

Parent-ego boundaries consist of all the activities we impose on our chil-dren that are not considered a core life skill. Learning a second language, playing an instrument, or participating in a sport are some common activities we sign our kids up for that would fall under parent-ego boundaries.

These activities are optional, but some parents tend to focus on their own ideas and ego when deciding what activities their child will do. When this occurs, children often perceive these boundaries as unfair and unjust. For example, parents may only allow their child to play a sport the parent enjoys, without considering if their child enjoys it too.

Parents who enforce parent-ego boundaries set expectations based on their own desires and rarely include the child in deciding what boundaries should be established. When children are forced to adhere to these types of boundaries, there is a greater risk for rebellious behaviors and conflict.

Instead of enforcing a parent-ego boundary, you can allow your child to have some input on the activity they choose to do. Also, consider the main reason you are establishing this type of boundary. For instance, you may be choosing a sport for your child to play because you want them to understand the importance of physical fitness for a healthy lifestyle. Wanting your child to be active is a great empowering boundary, but for them to enjoy it and make this a life-long habit, you need to take their preferences into account and let them choose a sport they enjoy doing.

Implementing Boundaries

Establishing healthy boundaries is similar to reinforcing positive behaviors in your child. There are several ways you can ensure boundaries are being upheld.

Effective Communication

When reinforcing boundaries, you want to remain calm and respectful to your child. They can express their opinion or disagree with the established boundaries, but they will still be expected to adhere to the boundaries in place. Yelling or belittling your child for trying to negotiate boundaries will not teach them to communicate their desires effectively. Instead, modeling calm and respectful behaviors as you communicate your expectations sets the foundation for children to learn how to communicate their own wants and desires clearly and calmly.

Family Rules

Family rules establish structure and help a child better understand behaviors that are acceptable and behaviors that are not tolerated. For example, acceptable behaviors include good manners like saying please and thank you. Hitting, screaming, or using unkind words are examples of behaviors that are not tolerated. Boundaries should be enforced in the same way. Go over rules and ensure your child understands what is off-limits, while also letting your child know that if they feel a rule is unfair they can respectfully speak to you about their feelings.

Use the following to help guide you in creating your own family rules:

1. Identify and define the family rule.

2. Explain the rule.

3. Everyone must follow the rules (children should not be the only ones who are expected to comply with family or house rules).

4. Explain consequences, and follow through with consequences when rules are not followed.

Keep in mind that your rules need to be explained to all adults who care for your child. Expectations should be the same no matter who your child is around and all adults should be on the same page with regards to expectations, consequences, and other disciplinary actions.

Be Concise

It can be easy to get caught up in over-explaining boundaries to your child. You want to be sure your child understands the rules in place and provide them with an opportunity to voice their opinions, but talking about the rules endlessly is not going to help them remember the information.

Younger children, especially, are not developmentally able to listen, retain, and make use of lengthy amounts of information. To implement boundaries effectively, give brief, concise directions. Keep it simple when you introduce the rules. Tell your child what is expected and the associated consequences. For example, you could state, "You need to clean up your toys before bedtime or we won't have time for your favorite bedtime story." If your child has not cleaned their room by bedtime, remind them, "Your room is not cleaned and it is bedtime now. That means we cannot read your favorite story tonight."

When instructions are straight and to the point, there is little room for arguing or conflict. Consistently following through on your boundaries will teach your child that the rules are nonnegotiable.

Be Consistent

If you implement boundaries inconsistently, you are teaching your child that the rules don't always apply to them and they don't always have to abide by them. It is easy to do what is convenient because there are many days where your energy and patience may run out and you become emotionally drained. However, remember that letting your child ignore boundaries now is only going to result in more conflict in the future.

Your child is not going to gracefully accept the consequences when they step out of line. They will be upset about those consequences, but you must follow through. Remember, allowing your child to experience emotions and learn that their actions have consequences is essential for them to develop the effective coping skills they will need later in life. Boundaries are what will keep your child safe, healthy, and happy in the long run.

Have Patience

Establishing boundaries can take time for everyone to get used to. Your child will probably not immediately be on board with new rules and systems. You need to allow time for your child to adjust and learn that certain behaviors are unacceptable, could be unsafe, and will be corrected through consequences. As with anything else, you need to commit to the boundaries and remind your child about the boundaries regularly until they begin to fully understand the new structure.

Recognize Your Child's Limitations

Children will also have their own boundaries that we, as parents, must also respect. If you expect your child to be considerate of other people's boundaries, then we need to model that by respecting their boundaries too. For instance, showing affection is a common boundary that young children often try to establish for themselves, but many parents ignore their request and urge, "Give your brother a hug," or "Give grandma a kiss goodbye." Your child should not be forced to show physical affection if they don't want to. They are likely not refusing out of spite, but instead are just telling you that they do not want to be affectionate at the moment.

Another limitation parents commonly ignore is when their child says they don't like something. For instance, your child may ask you to stop tickling them, but you continue to do so until they react in a negative way that results in a punishment for their behavior. You can probably see how this would be frustrating and confusing for a child. When your child asks you to stop doing something, do not disregard their request. Instead, respond to them by letting them know you have heard them, and you won't do it again.

We need to be aware of situations when we are tempted to dismiss our child's self-imposed boundaries and, if appropriate, ensure that we model respecting these boundaries.

Boundaries are an important part of raising well-adjusted children, but in order for those boundaries to work they must be communicated and understood. That means you need effective strategies that will encourage open dialogue between you and your child.

Parental Action Plan

Create a list of boundaries you would like to establish or change in your home. To do this, think of four to five boundaries in your family life that currently cause conflict or dispute. How many of these are empowering boundaries and how many are parent-ego boundaries? Can any of them be changed or let go of to resolve these conflicts?

Then, review these with your partner and child(ren)—even toddlers can be involved in the rulemaking process. Have other family members come up with a few boundaries of their own that you can all agree on.

Next, make a separate list with your partner of the parent-ego boundaries you want to avoid or reduce. Try to come up with empowering boundaries to replace them, if appropriate, or agree to remove unnecessary parent-ego boundaries entirely.

6

ENCOURAGE OPEN CONVERSATION

D o you ever feel like you and your child are speaking different languages? At times, it can feel like you have no idea what's going on in their heads. It's important to remember you aren't a mind reader—the best way to understand what your child is thinking is to ask. But in order for your child to feel comfortable sharing their thoughts, they need to know they can safely communicate their feelings. In this chapter, we'll look at the critical role communication plays in families and what you can do to encourage it.

Why Communication Is Important

It is just as important to establish a clear line of communication as it is to set boundaries. Children should feel comfortable bringing up concerns, problems, or things they are struggling with. If a child views their parents or caretakers as hostile or frightening because of harsh verbal or physical punishments, they will avoid conversation with them. A strong family unit encourages open communication where each person in the family feels respected and heard.

Positive communication between you and your child will help build a stronger parent-child relationship. This type of communication involves having discussions about a variety of topics, not just when there is conflict or a problem to be solved. There are a few key components to encouraging effective positive communication with your child.

Praise

When you catch your child doing something positive or displaying desired behaviors, praise them. Praise can come in many forms, such as:

- Verbally telling your child exactly what they did that you liked.

- Giving your child attention for positive behaviors.

- Giving hugs, high fives, or a simple pat on the shoulder or back.

Giving praise is not just about encouraging the right behaviors. Praise should also let your child know that you are paying attention to them, which is alternatively known as label praise. These types of praises are often unexpected because your child may just be doing something they typically do. For instance, your child may be reading instead of watching television while you prepare dinner. Let your child know that it is nice they are reading quietly as you make dinner. This unexpected moment creates a brief connection with your child and lets them know you are paying attention to them.

Be Present

Being present does not mean just physically being in the same room as your child. Being present means you are giving your child your full attention and actively interacting with them. When your child is talking to you, sincerely listen to what they are saying. Remove other distractions such as the phone or television and pause your other tasks to look at your child, which reinforces that you are listening to what they say.

Active listening shows your child that you hear and care about what they are saying. Using active listening techniques can help you reassure your child that you are present with them. Reflect on what your child is saying by repeating a short phrase that they have used. You can add to this phrase, ask questions, or gently correct any mispronunciation (for younger children).

Reflection can also be used to connect with how your child is feeling. For instance, your child is crying and looks sad. You can say to them, "I see that something is upsetting you."

Quality Time

Set aside specific time, whether daily or weekly, to connect and communicate with your child. Give them your undivided attention for that specific time and allow them to talk freely about what they want.

For younger children, this can be a special playtime. During this playtime, allow your child to direct the activity. As you play, you can show you approve of the way they are playing by mimicking what they are doing with their toys. Give out plenty of praise for their good behaviors and be enthusiastic about the time you are spending with them. During this time, ignore minor misbehaviors. Your special playtime should not be spent correcting or questioning your child. It is simply a time to have fun!

For older children, creating quality time can be harder but is still essential for connecting and learning about what is going on in their lives. During quality time with your preteen or teen, find new activities you can explore together. Be sure that this time is free from phones or other electronics. Ask questions about what is going on with your child's school, friends, and other activities, but don't push them to answer completely. You don't always need to find something to do; just blocking out 15 to 30 minutes to sit down and talk with your older child can let them know that you are still there when they need you and that you are interested in what is going on with them.

Communication Techniques by Age

Understanding the best way to communicate with your child needs to take their age into consideration. It will be hard for a toddler to communicate with you the same way a teenager does, and you shouldn't expect them to. Knowing how your child is likely to communicate according to their age will help you formulate effective strategies for clarifying expectations and rules.

Infant: Birth to 12 Months

An infant's primary mode of communication is through cries, body movement, facial expression, and sounds. Even though your baby is not able to verbally tell you what they want or need, you can still begin to encourage communication with your infant in a few ways.

- Be responsive to your baby's cries and facial expressions. When they smile at you, smile back. Provide them plenty of comfort.

- Label emotions. When a baby cries, tell them, "You are crying and sound upset. It must be time to eat." Or if your baby smiles at something you are doing, you could say, "You are smiling! You must like it when mommy/daddy makes that funny noise with the cars."

- Capture your infant's attention by exaggerating facial expressions, raising the pitch of your voice (which means the tone of your voice goes higher, not that your volume gets louder), or talking in a sing-song manner.

- Take advantage of face-to-face activities by talking, making different facial expressions, or singing.

- Tune into a baby's temperament. Some babies are content with being observers, while others would much rather have frequent interaction. Knowing how your baby prefers to interact will give you a better sense of how to communicate with them.

Toddler: One to Three Years of Age

Around a child's first birthday, they are beginning to be more vocal and expressive with the sounds that they make. They may or may not have begun to form words yet, but they are able to communicate their emotions through expressions and body movements. You can encourage communication with your toddler in several ways:

- Understand your toddler's predictable communication efforts. They will often use the same sound or gesture to indicate what they want. They may pat the front door to tell you they want to play outside, or point at the fridge when they are thirsty. It is important that you respond promptly to these gestures, even if they cannot have what they are asking for.

- Teach them how to expand on their one-word phrases or sounds. For instance, if your child says 'mmm' when eating, say, "Mmm, that yogurt tastes good." When your child says "milk" after taking a sip from their cup you can say "Milk. That's right, you are drinking milk."

- Label their emotions. When you see they are having fun, say "Playing with your fire trucks makes you happy."

- Use daily routines as a time to talk through sequences of events. For example, when getting ready to leave the house you might say, "First we put our socks and shoes on, then we put on our coats, and now we are ready to go outside."

- Use a lot of descriptive words during playtime and follow your child's lead in how to play with them.

- Older toddlers can begin to understand simple, one-step directions. When giving direction, be clear about what you want your child to do and why they need to do it. You might say something like, "Bring me your cup. It's time to fill it with more water." This is also the age when you can start giving warnings about transitions, such as, "We have 10 more minutes to play at the park and then we need to go home to start making dinner." Be sure to give them two or three warnings when one activity is ending and another needs to begin.

Preschool and Kindergarten: Three to Five Years of Age

Most preschool-age children can talk in sentences and are usually eager to talk about things they have done. Children at this age begin to understand different forms of communication, such as verbal, written, and visual. You can encourage your child to communicate in the following ways:

- When you notice your child talking to themselves as they do an activity, leave them alone. For instance, they may be talking themselves through how to put a puzzle together with phrases like, "Does this piece go here? Maybe if I turn the other way? No, that piece doesn't match." Talking to themselves helps many young children maintain their focus on what they are doing. Once they have finished the activity, you can praise them for problem-solving and working through the challenges on their own.

- Ask your child questions about what they did during the day. Even if you were home together all day, you can still ask things like, "Do you remember what we did before your nap?" or "What was your favorite food you ate for lunch?"

- Encourage pretend or fantasy play.

- Continue to encourage your child to express their feelings. Also, ask them why they are feeling that way (whether the emotion is positive or negative).

School Age: 6 to 12 Years of Age

School-age children speak in full sentences and begin to ask a lot more questions. Your child will have many more opportunities to communicate at this age. You can encourage them to use effective and appropriate communication by considering the following:

- Have regular discussions about your child's friends. Ask what they have in common, what they dislike about other peers, and what activities they tend to do with their friends at school.

- Take advantage of opportunities for your child to use their problem-solving skills and help them set regular, realistic goals. For instance, your child may have a softball game over the weekend but also needs to study for a test on Monday. Ask your child when they plan to study for the test and discuss strategies for managing their time so your child has options, and help them (as needed) to choose the best one.

- Correct behaviors by explaining what was wrong with their actions, and why. Help your child understand the connection between their behavior and how it makes others feel.

- Begin to encourage proper conflict management. At this age, kids are often best friends one day and enemies the next. You can help your child navigate these bumps in their peer relationships by discussing or acting out interactions they've had (or have seen their peers have) that resulted in conflict. Help your child identify the best ways to resolve these conflicts while still being able to maintain the friendship.

Adolescents: 13 to 18 Years of Age

Many parents feel disconnected from their teens because this is the age when their child finds new independence. However, during these years communication is still essential, as your child will likely encounter some adult situations. Teens are notorious for acting on impulse, and because hormones also come into play their ability to regulate their emotions is not always the strongest. This puts them at a higher risk of making poor choices.

Maintaining a healthy parent-child relationship with your teen becomes even more important as they get older, but it doesn't get easier. First, remember what it was like when you were a teenager. It's a difficult time, and remaining understanding will help you stay calm and available to your child when they need you. However, during these years your teen will most likely be pulling away from wanting to talk to you and you may feel like you are talking to a wall when you try to get your teen to communicate with you. This can be frustrating when you are desperately trying to stay connected and involved in your child's life.

It is important to remain patient with your child. Do not pressure them to share information if they don't feel like it. If you maintain an open line of communication, your teen will most likely come to you to talk when they are ready. To help keep the lines of communication open, try the following suggestions:

- When your teen does come to you to talk, listen. Many times, teens just need to feel like someone hears them; they don't always need advice or to be told what to do. Many kids will open up more if they know their parents aren't just trying to pry information from them. Be present and simply hear what they have to say.

- Don't downplay their feelings. One reason teens avoid going to their parents when they are dealing with big emotions is because they want to feel like they are understood. For instance, if your child comes to you upset and disappointed about not making the soccer team, it can be natural to tell them that they can always try next year or that they can play another sport. In reality, your teen may need you to empathize that it is super upsetting that they didn't make the team, especially because you know they put in a lot of hard work. Validating your child's feelings, even if you disagree with them, will help keep you connected with your child.

- Allow your teen to earn your trust, and then find ways to tell or show your teen that you trust them. When you let your teen know that you have faith in them, it boosts their confidence and they will make good choices more often. Remember they still need your approval and praise, so find ways to tell them that they are doing a good job.

- Remain in control of your own emotions. Your teen is still learning how to control their emotions and, while it is frustrating that they may treat you unkindly, it is best to keep your own temper under control. It is okay to take a break from one another if you are in a heated argument or conflict. Pause the discussion until you are both able to return to the topic calmly.

Finally, observe your child. They may not be verbally telling you that something is going on, but often they will show you. If your teen is more distant from family and friends, if they have cut back on doing things they enjoy, or if there is a change in their mood, appetite, or energy, ask them if there is something they need to talk about. These are clear nonverbal signs that your teen is probably struggling and if they do not feel comfortable talking to you, you can suggest they talk to someone else. Reassure your child that you are there to listen—not judge, criticize, or even tell them what they should do.

Improving Communications

Proper communication is a skill that can be developed and improved upon. If you feel you can benefit from becoming a more effective communicator, take note of the following tips.

Active Listening

As previously mentioned, active listening is a way you can connect and show you are interested in your child at any age. Active listening is essential for effective communication. Some ways you can incorporate active listening when communicating with your child include:

- Be aware of your body language. Face your child when they are talking with you and make eye contact.

- Be aware of their body language. Communication is not just about what is being said verbally. Pay attention to the nonverbal cues your child may be giving that will help you understand what they are feeling or trying to explain.

- Try not to interrupt your child; even when they pause to find the right words to say, allow them to finish their own sentences.

- Don't immediately assume that if your child is sharing a problem, they want you to help solve it. Many times, children just need someone to listen to them so they can gain clarity about what they need to do to solve the problem themselves.

- Show your child you are interested in what they are saying by repeating phrases or asking them to tell you more about a specific idea.

- Encourage your child to describe what they are feeling.

Encourage Open Communication

Proper communication is something that should be modeled by all family members. The family unit as a whole plays a vital role in teaching children how to function in the world. A family that is supportive, warm, and loving provides essential support for a growing child. A strong family unit exhibits strong communication skills.

Good communication means that everyone in the family feels they are able to voice their opinions, be heard, and be received with respect. Improving communication among the whole family will model for your child how they can become better at communicating their needs, wants, and emotions. Some ways you can begin to encourage more open communication in your home include:

- Encourage all family members to share their thoughts and feelings. Model being respectful of each person's feelings and thoughts.

- Create family rituals that focus on quality time together. This means you are doing activities together, not just sitting in front of the television. Dedicated family time can include sitting down for dinner as a family or going for a walk together. Be sure that this time is clearly defined as family time and that no other interruptions occur.

- When someone is talking to you, give them your full attention.

- Do not listen to react; listen to hear and understand what the other person is saying.

- Before giving advice, ensure that you fully understand the problem the other person is struggling with.

- Encourage everyone to use 'I' statements instead of 'you' statements. An 'I' statement says, "I don't like when you grab things without asking because then I can't find things when I need them and it makes me angry" instead of, "You always take things that don't belong to you and you never put things back. It is inconsiderate of you!" Using 'I' statements expresses your feelings and emotions clearly without shaming or guilting the other family member.

- When conflict in the family arises, work through it together. Focus on finding solutions for any problems as opposed to criticizing and judging each other for their part in the conflict.

Coach Your Child Through Big Emotions

Help your child understand what they feel. By coaching your child how to label and understand their emotions, you not only begin to teach them to self-regulate, but you also strengthen your emotional bond with them. Children who grow up in households with families who proactively talk about their feelings have been shown to perform better academically, build healthier and stronger relationships with others, handle challenging social situations, and have less preventable diseases than children who grow up in homes where feelings are not discussed openly (Gable, 2016).

To help you become a successful emotional coach for your child, practice the following tips:

- Be observant of your child's emotions.

- Take advantage of your child's emotional expressions to kick-start communication about what they are feeling.

- Do not keep emotional labels broad and overly generic. Teach your child different labels to specifically express what they are feeling. For example, instead of using a general word like 'happy,' teach your child to describe their feelings as joyful, ecstatic, excited, or content. By understanding that there is more than one way to describe what they feel, your child will learn how to gauge their emotions with more accuracy.

- Guide your child through problem-solving techniques to help them manage big emotions. When they are frustrated, remind them to pause, take a breath, and walk away to give them space from what is frustrating them.

Be Mindful of Your Wording

The words you use with your child will have a huge impact on their behavior, your connection with them, and their self-confidence. It is not uncommon for parents to forget that they are speaking to their loved, amazing little child when they are frustrated about behavior. This can result in using hurtful words and phrases that you regret saying once the frustration has cooled.

Be aware of allowing labels or unkind words to enter the conversation with your child. Sometimes parents will unintentionally call their child names, and there are many instances where unkind words might be used to express frustration or disappointment. Labeling your child by saying a phrase like "you're being bad" only makes your child feel negatively about themselves and has no positive impact on their behavior. Additionally, unkind words or phrases like "that was a stupid choice" are also unhelpful.

Many parents also tend to use the word 'don't' too much. Instead, get into the habit of focusing on the 'do's' rather than the 'don'ts.' When we want a child to stop behaviors, we often tell them what not to do. However, this does not provide them with a better alternative. Instead, using 'don't' statements tends to reinforce the negative behavior because that is what it focuses on. Rewording your statements slightly can help reinforce appropriate behaviors. Instead of saying, "Don't run in the house," try saying, "Remember to walk in the house." Turn the statement, "Don't color on the walls," into the statement, "We only color on paper."

It is clear that communication between you and your child needs to happen regularly, and it's something that can take time to develop. But what do you do in the moments when calm communication isn't easy? What's the best way to handle conflict?

Parental Action Plan

Look for opportunities this week to connect with your child through one-on-one play. If you regularly journal, consider scheduling this time in advance and then write about the activities you did with your child and the connection that was created.

Practice active listening the next time you and your child talk.

7

HANDLE CONFLICT IN THE MOMENT

Wouldn't it be nice if you never had to deal with disagreements, arguments, or talking back? Unfortunately, conflict is a natural and unavoidable part of any relationship. However, that doesn't mean it needs to poison the relationship you have with your child. Keep reading to discover how to manage and contain conflict in the moment.

Conflict Management

Conflict is inevitable, but that does not mean you have to sit and passively allow it to unfold and escalate. As a parent, you will find yourself in conflict with your child starting from the toddler years and continuing throughout the teenage years. Learning how to remain in control of your own emotions while positively reacting to theirs is no easy task, but it is possible to remain open-minded and find a resolution like a pro.

As your child grows, you will notice you encounter more conflict. You may have to fight with your toddler to go to bed or eat their vegetables, but these minor conflicts are preparing you for the disagreements you will face with your teenager. Preteens and teenagers are testing their limits. They want to have more freedom, and they are more vocal about their opinions, preferences, and wants.

It is vital that we learn to handle conflict in a constructive manner. Effective conflict management will:

- Reduce family stress

- Maintain and strengthen your relationship with your child

- Allow you and your child to consider each other's perspective

- Give your child an opportunity to learn and practice life skills, like negotiating and compromising

Remain Fair

Handling conflict needs to take everyone's feelings into consideration. When your child feels as though their voice is being heard and their feelings are acknowledged, they will be more willing to discuss the best way to handle the situation. Remaining fair means you are not enforcing a consequence just because you say so; instead, you give your child an opportunity to use and strengthen their ability to manage themselves, with guidance depending on age. Additionally, you can approach conflicts with your child in a fair manner when you remember the following:

- Focus on the current behavior or problem.

- Rely on problem-solving skills that you can teach your child. Encourage your child to come up with strategies on their own to address the problem.

- Provide opportunities for your child to earn your trust. Additionally, show your child that you can be trusted too. Encourage fami-

RAISING POSITIVE LITTLE PEOPLE

ly members to practice forgiveness. Model the right behaviors, use the words "I'm sorry," and admit when you are wrong.

Handling Tantrums

They happen out of nowhere. Sometimes you may be able to brace yourself as you notice your little one begin to scrunch up their face, bite their lower lip, or stomp their tiny foot with the force of a wrecking ball. You're facing what every parent dreads: the tantrum.

This explosion of anger, frustration, and utter chaos is accompanied by screaming, flopping on the floor like a fish out of water, or watching your child take off at a speed you never knew they could travel. Parents try to avoid tantrums at all costs, and do everything they can to stop them once they start.

However, these fits of anger are a normal part of your child's development. Instead of trying to prevent them, it is better to understand why your little one is melting down at that moment. Tantrums can happen for many reasons and are most common among children between the ages of one and three. At this age, children become easily overwhelmed by big emotions that they either haven't dealt with before or haven't learned how to express appropriately.

Older children can also have tantrums, often due to the child not knowing how to safely express their emotions. Some children may also struggle with managing their emotions and have not learned coping mechanisms to calm their little bodies and minds, so they throw a tantrum instead.

Minimize the Frequency of Tantrums

Since many tantrums can be avoided if a child has all their basic needs met, it is important that your child gets enough sleep, is offered regular meals and healthy snacks, and receives plenty of attention. Once you are sure these basic needs can be ruled out, you can begin to identify more specific situations that seem to regularly trigger a tantrum.

Take notice of what external factors reappear when your child has a tantrum. Note similarities such as time of day, place, clothing, sounds, or weather. If you can identify patterns to your child's tantrums, you can begin to create a plan to help your child effectively cope with their big feelings. Other suggestions that can help decrease the frequency of tantrums include:

- Younger children will often lack the words to properly communicate their wants and needs, which is a common trigger for tantrums. Find ways to help your child communicate, such as by pointing at what they want, using simple sign language to express 'want,' 'more,' 'play,' 'eat,' 'drink,' and 'all done,' and giving them visuals or pictures that they can use to indicate what they want.

- Allow your child to make age-appropriate choices. You can give your toddler two or three options and let them choose which shirt they want to wear. Let them decide what fruit they want for a snack, or with their lunch. Giving your child appropriate options and letting them make the choice helps them feel more independent and in control over some aspects of their life.

- Before you immediately say 'no' to a request, consider if it is unreasonable for you to accommodate them. For instance, your child went through their bedtime routine without complaining or needing to be prompted and then asks for an extra bedtime story. While this deviates from your typical one-story-at-bedtime routine, your child did comply with all the evening expectations and you may decide this is a reasonable request.

- Recognize when your child is about to have a tantrum and step in to de-escalate the situation before it goes any further.

- Encourage your child to use their words to communicate their wants and needs, and praise them every time they try.

- Have a reward system set up for when your child appropriately uses their words as opposed to screaming, kicking, or throwing things.

When tantrums do occur, remember to remain calm. The more frustrated you become, the more frustrated your child will become.

Effective Strategies to Handle Tantrums at Home

Tantrums are more likely to occur at home, and these can often be more predictable and easier to handle than public tantrums. Some ways to help your child cope with their big emotions include:

- Always remain calm. Remember, you want to model the behaviors you expect them to learn.

- If your child is having a tantrum because they are not getting something they want, do not give in to their demands once they have calmed down. Tantrums should not be a way for your child to get what they want or to get out of doing something they don't want to do.

- Know what works for your child in terms of helping them calm down. Some children need a quiet space to regain control of their little bodies, while others will feel more anxious if they are left alone. Once your child is calm, comfort them and reassure them that they are safe.

- Use distraction to redirect their behaviors. This can be incredibly effective with younger children.

- If you feel you are unable to maintain control of your emotions, walk away. Place your child in a safe space and give yourself time to calm your own emotions.

- Maintain consistent routines. You should avoid making changes to the household routine just to avoid tantrums. Remember, your child will learn to regulate themselves and will learn appropriate ways to communicate their feelings when expectations remain consistent.

If you find that the tantrums do not seem to diminish or last a long time, you may want to bring this up with your child's pediatrician. Sometimes tantrums can be the result of something other than big emotions or frustration over poor communication. Sensory issues can lead to out-of-control tantrums where nothing calms your child. Speaking to a medical professional can steer you in the right direction for how to help your child, if there is an underlying medical concern.

Effective Strategies to Handle Tantrums in Public

Tantrums out in public are embarrassing, and many parents become more frustrated at their child's behavior if they worry the people around them are judging them and making comments about their ability to parent. This usually results in parents desperately doing whatever they have to do to get their child to quiet down, which only provides fuel for the next public outing. Despite the extra stress of tantrums outside of the home, there are a few effective ways you can encourage your child to express their feelings in a more suitable manner:

- Go over expectations before you reach your destination. If you are going grocery shopping, review the grocery-store rules with your child and tell them what the consequences are for misbehaving. Have a reward in place for positive behaviors. For instance, you can explain to your child that while you are at the grocery store, they need to sit in the cart (or hold your hand) the entire time. They are not to reach for things on the shelf or throw things into the cart. They are to use a quiet, inside voice. If they are warned three times about their behavior, then you will need to leave the store without getting everything on the list. If they cooperate and you get the shopping done quickly, then you will have time to briefly stop at the playground on the way home, or they can help make their favorite meal for dinner.

- It is important to remind yourself that the people you worry are judging you at the store can actually most likely relate to what you are going through. Nearly all parents experience a public tantrum at some point, so those looks of 'judgment' might actually be looks of understanding and empathy.

- Stay calm and avoid yelling at or threatening your child. Your child won't learn how to better manage their big emotions if you can't manage your own.

- Remember to stick with your plan. If your child begins to have a tantrum and it becomes serious or drawn out, leave the store. You can either go home and finish your shopping later, or give your child an opportunity to sit in the car and calm down before trying to finish the shopping. Go over the expectations again before you return to the store.

Negotiating or Staying Firm

While there are benefits to teaching your child how to negotiate to get what they want, this is not always an option. Recognize when negotiation is off the table and how to handle frustration from your child when they realize they aren't going to get what they want. If your child is having a tantrum because of an empowering boundary imposed on them, you must remain firm. Remember, if you are acting in your child's best interest, no compromises should be made when tantrums arise. There are various techniques you can turn to, depending on your child's age, to help resolve conflicts regarding negotiating and standing firm.

Negotiating with Toddlers and School-Age Kids

It is understandable why many parents want to negotiate with their children. They try to beg, bribe, or coax their child to get them to listen and behave appropriately. While there are some instances when negotiation may be effective, in most situations this approach is not sustainable or helpful.

Instead of negotiating, parents should consider the following techniques:

- The interest-based approach is best suited for younger children because it takes into consideration that they can be more emotional and not as rational as older children. The interest-based approach helps you understand the real reason your child is being uncooperative. For instance, your child is digging a big hole in the front yard. You could immediately yell at them and send them inside, or you could ask what they are trying to accomplish. Maybe they are trying to make a garden like their grandmother has at her house, or they want to plant pretty flowers to make you happy. You can then come up with a plan where your child can use a small area of the yard for a garden, or get a container and allow them to use that as their 'garden.' By understanding your child's underlying goal, you can come up with a plan that makes both of you happy.

- Stress-reducers help eliminate other factors that can make tantrums worse and lead to more conflict around decision-making. This means looking at your child's daily activities and making adjustments where needed. For instance, a tired child who throws a tantrum in the early morning because they are too tired to get up will benefit from having an earlier bedtime. A toddler who becomes overwhelmed when deciding what to wear every day may need to have fewer options to choose from, or may need to decide ahead of time to eliminate the battle. Stress-reducers give your child more time to make decisions on their own.

- Being empathetic instead of frustrated or angry with your child in moments of conflict can help your child feel understood and result in more cooperation. Showing empathy means you actively listen to your child when they are trying to communicate the cause of their big emotions. Asking open-ended questions lets you clarify what is causing your child's issues, and paraphrasing reassures your child that you are listening and doing your best to be supportive. When using this approach, get down on your child's level. This helps your child feel more secure and lets you talk with them face-to-face instead of looking down at them.

When used appropriately, negotiating with younger children can be a way for parents and children to build trust. It can also be used to help resolve conflict, because the child gets to feel like they've had a say too. Negotiating is not just about giving your child what they want. You can still establish limitations and consequences.

Negotiating with Preteens and Teens

As children grow older, negotiating can be a more effective strategy. Negotiation with your preteen or teenager can:

- Teach your child to think through their wants and needs

- Teach your child to communicate their wants and needs in an appropriate and reasonable manner

- Teach your child to see things from other people's perspective

- Teach them how to compromise

- Teach good decision-making skills

However, negotiating with preteens and teenagers can also backfire if parents feel they are spending too much time negotiating simple requests and start to think their child is manipulating them. It is important to prepare ahead of time when you begin negotiating with your older children. There are certain things that most children will try to negotiate, such as staying up or out later, borrowing money, and dating.

If you are not prepared to negotiate, you can tell your teenager that you need time to think about what they are asking for—or in some cases, just tell you what they are doing. For instance, your teen may say, "On Saturday, I am going to Jacob's house," instead of asking if they can go. Choose a time when you and your teen can sit down and discuss their request. Be sure to keep your word about when you will have the discussion, or your child will lose trust in you.

Whether you have had time to prepare for negotiation or not, all back-and-forth discussions should check off three simple steps.

1. *You take turns listening and talking, with the goal being to come up with a compromise.*

Remain calm when discussing your child's wants, but keep your tone firm when it needs to be. Actively listen to your child. Let them say what they need to say without interruption. When your child has had their chance to speak, ask questions to clarify things if necessary. When you express your views, do so in a way that leaves room for further discussion. For instance, if your child wants to go to their friend's house on Saturday, you could say, "I don't mind that you want to go to your friend's, but we are having dinner at grandma's for her birthday that day and I would like you to be here to help decorate the cake or wrap gifts. What time are you planning on going and what will you two be doing?" By stating your concerns and allowing your child to help come up with a plan that satisfies everyone, there should be less frustration around negotiating a compromise.

Not all negotiations will run smoothly, and the conversation can become intense. In these situations, be sure to recognize when the conversation is getting too heated or when the hope of a compromise is at a standstill. Tell your child that you need a break and that you can continue the conversation a little later in the day, such as after dinner.

1. *You both accept the final decision.*

When trying to come to an agreement, let your child know what is not negotiable. This will often depend on how mature your child is, their personality, the amount of trust you have with your child, and factors that are specific to the current situation. For instance, if you do not want your child walking home when it's dark out, you will need to pick them up if they want to stay out after dark.

Be sure to have options for your child to consider during the negotiation. Also show that you are willing to hear their ideas for reaching a compromise. Be firm about your non-negotiables, however.

1. *You establish the next steps.*

When a decision has been made, be sure that you both understand what is expected. Restate what you have both agreed on and let your child accept the discussion. Established consequences should also be clarified and your child should agree to them. When the decision and consequences have been reviewed and understood, remember to give your child praise. Thank them for working with you to come to a compromise and tell them how mature they are.

When You Should Remain Firm

There are certain times where the answer is going to be 'no,' no matter how much your child tries to beg, plead, and get you to change your mind. For instance, the time your child needs to be in bed may be nonnegotiable. Where you let your child go without adult supervision is nonnegotiable.

Negotiations are acceptable when you admit that your child has come to you with a solution that you are willing to let them try. However, you may have asked for some time to think about your answer and after thinking about it, you are still more comfortable saying 'no.' For example, your child's friend has just gotten their driver's license and your child wants to go to the beach with them over the weekend. The friend will be driving and the beach is two hours away. At first, you do not think it is a bad idea. The friend is responsible, but they are still a new driver and this will be the first long drive they take by themselves. You may ultimately not feel comfortable allowing your child and their friend to drive all the way to the beach, but you have no problem with them finding a place closer to home to go to.

Additionally, there are some things that you won't waver on because they are firm family or household rules. For example, your child asks to skip doing their chores for the day so they can go out with their friends because it is their best friend's birthday. In this case, the child is asking for an exception to a household rule. If your child is asking to push the limits of an established family or household rule, then you need to remain firm in your response.

Additional Tips for Managing Conflict

There are an assortment of helpful tips that can minimize conflict during negotiation and other challenging situations with your child. These tips can be used or modified regardless of your child's age.

- Be clear about the goal and what you expect and want from your child. Don't bring up the past. If you are able to prepare for negotiations ahead of time, write your goals down. This will help you and your child stay on topic when you sit down to talk.

- Come up with a plan of action with your child. You can begin to gather information and have a few options to suggest to your child, but let them come up with their own ideas as well.

- Seek advice from others. Not every negotiation is going to be easy to navigate. It is wise to ask others for their opinions and solicit advice for navigating difficult situations with your child. Friends, family members, and even professionals can provide you with ways to clarify your goals and create an effective action plan for your child.

- Use good timing. Don't try to force your child to talk when they aren't ready. Select a time to talk with your child when there will be no distractions and you won't have to rush through the conversation.

- Pick a place to sit down and discuss the problems. Depending on the topic of discussion, it is vital to choose the right location where your child feels comfortable and safe talking through the problem.

- Prepare for your child's reaction. If possible, imagine how you want the conversation with your child to go. Imagine all the ways your child might respond to the limitation or consequences. Rehearse your responses to anticipate your reaction. The idea is to be prepared for both the best-case and the worst-case scenario.

- Acknowledge your own responsibilities. While it can be easy to blame your child for misbehavior, consider your role in their behavior. If you have not been consistent with consequences or have been lenient with boundaries, it is understandable that your child may not act appropriately or fight with you more about getting what they want. Admit when you have made mistakes and what you could have done differently.

- Give your child a chance to speak their mind. While you may already be set on your answer, you still want to give your child a chance to be heard. Remain respectful and attentive to what they say. Your child may bring up valid points for their argument and this may cause you to consider compromising a little more. Unless it is a nonnegotiable, be open to give a little and compromise.

- Most importantly, remain calm, respectful, and understanding, especially when you do need to say 'no.' This cannot be stressed enough: negotiating and resolving conflict is not going to be easy. Sometimes things might go smoothly, but other times will require you to remain in control of your own emotions and behaviors.

A big part of managing conflict successfully comes from managing your own emotional response as well, which isn't always easy. In the next chapter, we'll look at strategies that can be used in all aspects of life to practice mindfulness and emotional acceptance.

Parental Action Plan

The next time you deal with a tantrum or conflict with your child, use a journal after the event to reflect on how you handled the situation. Did you allow for negotiating when you should have stood firm? Did you remain calm and count to 10 before reacting? Be specific about what caused the conflict and what resulted afterward. Over time, this practice will help you assess how you are feeling and what emotions you need to manage in these difficult moments.

8

ALWAYS BE MINDFUL

I understand that mindfulness is not for everyone. Some may not see the benefits of mindfulness for parenting; if this is you, feel free to skip to chapter 9. However, this is a practice I use, and I believe in the scientifically supported and firsthand benefits I have seen from using mindfulness. Mindfulness does not involve sitting in a room for hours meditating. Instead, it involves responding to your children consciously and attentively, as opposed to reactively or emotionally.

What Is Mindful Parenting?

Mindfulness has been shown to help reduce and manage stress. It is a practice that can help you remain present with your children, understand your own emotions and thoughts better, and accept your experiences without judgment. Through mindfulness practices, you learn that you have more control over how you react to a situation and interact with your child.

When you become mindful, you are allowing yourself to pause before you react. This is essential for modeling constructive behaviors for your children. Mindfulness also helps you to take a step back from the situation and recognize your thoughts as simply thoughts, rather than as realities. You can then better assess the current situation as it really is, because you can distance yourself from unhelpful thoughts and emotions.

Learning how to remain in control despite what you are feeling or thinking is empowering. You remain the calm parent your child needs.

Benefits of Mindful Parenting

As parents, mindfulness allows us to focus on what is happening in the present moment. Through practice, you can bring more awareness to any situation at any time. As a result, you make a conscious choice as to how you remain present with your child, even through times of conflict.

Numerous studies have shown that those who incorporate mindfulness practices through their day experience less stress, have better health, and are able to bounce back from difficulties more easily than those who do not practice mindfulness ("What Is Mindful Parenting?," n.d.). When it comes to parenting, mindful parents approach their kids with a more positive mindset. This leads to more positive interactions, including productive conversations around emotions and behaviors.

Children who are taught mindfulness techniques are able to notice their emotions without having to immediately react to them. They are calmer, more focused, and can concentrate better after they have learned how to control their thoughts and emotions. A child who learns how to use mindfulness throughout their day will be able to manage their stress properly and develop vital skills that help them balance all areas of their life as they get older.

Children with parents who practice mindfulness may develop better social and decision-making skills. Recent research has shown that children of mindful parents not only understand their emotions better, but can accept their emotions without letting them dictate their behaviors (Marcin, 2019).

Additional benefits of mindfulness include:

- Strengthens the parent-child relationship

- Improves communication

- Reduces aggressive behaviors (for both parent and child)

- Reduces the risk of depression and anxiety

- Lessens conflict

How to Practice Mindful Parenting

Mindful parenting incorporates mindfulness principles into your parenting style. Mindful parents take the time to see things from their child's perspective so they can accept the positive and negative emotions their child is struggling with. By doing this, you have a better understanding and are reminded that children see the world differently because they live in the moment. Mindful parenting focuses on:

- Bringing awareness to and maintaining attention in the present moment

- Intentionally understanding your behaviors and your child's behaviors

- Having a positive attitude, which eliminates judgments and instead allows room for compassion and acceptance

To become a more mindful parent, you must:

- Listen and observe the situation without judgment. Take everything in, from what your child is saying (both verbally and non-verbally) to what you notice in your surroundings, by relying on and tuning into your senses.

- Approach situations for what they are. You need to detach emotion from the situation and let go of unrealistic expectations.

- Strengthen your emotional awareness. This means you are aware of the interaction that goes from you to your child and from your child back to you. Emotional awareness allows you to identify which emotions are affecting the situation and whether they are new emotions that are specific to the current situation, or emotions stemming from past experiences that you have attached to the situation.

- Maintain control of your reactions instead of allowing your emotions to drive them.

- Have compassion for your child, even if you do not agree with their behavior. This includes being empathetic to show you understand and hear your child as well as letting go of any self-blame you may be burdened with.

To become a mindful parent, begin by identifying what triggers you to react immediately in certain situations. Acknowledge your own feelings when you are encountering conflict with your child. Question what is really causing these reactions. Are they due to a past experience, childhood upbringing, or something else? When you become more aware of your own emotions and what is driving them, you will learn how to disengage from these emotions and remain present with your child.

Breath work and the STOP method are two simple ways you can strengthen your mindfulness skills. Breath work involves bringing awareness to your breathing. Take a deep breath. Focus on drawing your breath in to fill your lungs and diaphragm. Then, concentrate on allowing the breath to escape slowly. Now, label what you are feeling but do not react to it—for instance, "I am feeling angry." If you notice your body begin to react to the emotion or feeling, draw in another deep breath and exhale slowly.

The STOP method provides you with a useful acronym to use in any emotionally charged situation. When you stop, you:

- Stop

- Take a deep breath

- Observe your thoughts and emotions

- Proceed to respond to your child with a calm and clear state of mind

Being Mindful Throughout the Day

Practicing mindfulness throughout the day will allow you to better utilize your skills in moments of conflict and stress. A few ways you can be more mindful throughout the day include:

- Actively listening. Turn your attention to the person who is talking to you and engage in the conversation with intent. Remember, listen to understand—not just to hear their words.

- Accept yourself and your child without judgment. This means you acknowledge feelings without becoming overwhelmed by them.

- Visualize yourself in your child's shoes and connect with what they are feeling. How do they need you to respond? Consider how you would want someone to respond to your emotions if you were feeling what your child is feeling. Match your response to your child accordingly.

- Manage your own feelings and emotions in stressful situations. Learn to pause when you feel negative emotions.

- Show compassion to yourself and your child. Practice self-care and self-compassion.

As you practice managing your own emotions, remember that your child is also learning to manage and express theirs. It is essential that you acknowledge and validate their feelings so they know they are heard. As a result, it is more likely that they'll listen to you or at least consider your perspective.

Parental Action Steps

Choose one of the following mindfulness practices to begin today. You can do this on your own or invite your kids to join you.

1. *Mindful self-compassion*

This practice is useful when you are dealing with strong emotions and you are becoming overwhelmed with negative thoughts and self-criticism.

Begin by inhaling and slowly exhaling a few times. Close your eyes, bring your attention to the emotions you are feeling, and label them. Shift your focus to how your body feels. Start at the crown of your head and slowly move down to your feet while mentally noting where you feel tightness, pain, or discomfort. Next, place your hands over your heart, take a deep breath in, and slowly exhale. Imagine a warm, glowing light forming around you that resonates from your heart. Intentionally shift to kind thoughts. If it helps, consider what you would say to a friend who turned to you for support. Allow yourself to bask in this warming golden light. Take a few more deep breaths, lower your hands, and relax the body. Then open your eyes.

1. *Mindfulness movement*

Mindfulness movement can take many forms and is a great activity to do with your kids. You can turn on instrumental music and allow your body to move with the music. Yoga is another ideal form of mindfulness movement.

You can try mindful movement by simply stretching. Stand up tall and breathe in through your nose. Slowly inhale as you lift your arms and stretch them up over your head. Bring the palms together. Now, slowly begin to exhale through your mouth and turn the palms out away from your body as you slowly lower your arms down to your sides. Continue to stretch your arms and hands by reaching down to the floor.Repeat this movement along with the slow inhale/exhale two more times, or until your body and mind feel completely relaxed and calm.

1. *4, 5, 6 Breathing*

This is a mindful breathing exercise that helps you release stress and restore calmness and clarity to your thoughts.

To begin, inhale and fill your abdomen with air. Exhale through your mouth. On your next inhale, breathe in for a count of four through your nose. Hold your breath for a count of five, then exhale for a count of six. Repeat this three times.

Once you are done, take note of how you feel emotionally and physically.

9

VALIDATE THEIR FEELINGS

V alidation is one of the most important things you can do for your child for a myriad of reasons. Keep reading to discover what these reasons are and how you can practice validation.

The Role of Validation

Validation helps kids feel heard and understood. Children should be encouraged to express their emotions in appropriate ways to promote a better sense of self, build confidence, and create a stronger connection with parents or caregivers.

Validation means we recognize and accept that our child has their own feelings, thoughts, and opinions—which to them feel very real and are very true. As parents, we often disregard our children's emotions and feelings because to us, they may not make logical sense. We have a more advanced way of sorting through our thoughts and feelings, whereas young children are still learning to comprehend theirs.

Validation is not the same as providing praise or comfort. When you give praise, you are encouraging desired behaviors. When you give comfort, you provide your child with a safe space to experience their uncomfortable emotions. Validation, on the other hand, is about acknowledging what your child is experiencing—whether it is negative or positive—and how they respond to these experiences.

When you provide validation, you encourage your child to remain open and share their thoughts and feelings. Your goal is to do this without judgment, criticism, or making your child feel alone or abandoned. Validation is beneficial for child development and the parent-child relationship in a few ways:

- Validation helps de-escalate intense and emotionally charged situations. Validating a child's emotion helps reduce its intensity, which will help your child regain control of themselves faster. Once they are more calm, you can further help your child by suggesting possible solutions to what is causing them to experience such intense emotions. As a result, your child learns how to rationally consider what to do next instead of letting their emotions control how they behave.

- Validation provides an opportunity to teach children to label their emotions appropriately. Children need to learn how to label what they are feeling instead of lashing out with negative words or physical aggression. Communicating their feelings appropriately lets the adults around them react calmly and provide the right support for the child. Having these kinds of educational, calm interactions with your child will also lead to a stronger parent-child relationship.

- Validation helps build up your child's frustration tolerance. You can use validation to praise your child for how hard they are working on a difficult task, or for completing a challenging task despite how long and hard it was. When we validate their behaviors and let them know we recognize how frustrating it must have been at times, we encourage them to repeat those same behaviors in the future.

Separating Feelings From Reactions

Validating your child requires making a distinction between their feelings and their reactions. You should never tell a child that what they are feeling is wrong. Even adults may have misguided feelings when in certain situations, and it is no different for a child. Feelings should never be discredited. However, your child's actions can be unacceptable.

For example, your child may become angry with you when you tell them 'No,' and hit you out of frustration. In this scenario, their anger is understandable but hitting is not an appropriate reaction to their angry feelings. To practice appropriate validation, remind your child that while they are allowed to be mad, they are not allowed to hurt others because they are mad. You can validate their anger, as they aren't wrong to feel mad, but you should still enforce consequences for their behavior, because hitting is an inappropriate response to anger.

Unintentionally Invalidating Your Child

Parents may inadvertently invalidate their child's feelings. This means the child's emotional response is judged, criticized, or ignored, or the child is simply told they are wrong for feeling how they feel.

Invalidation can occur when you try to calm your child. How many times have you told your child everything is going to be okay when they are upset? How many times have you jumped right into providing advice or solutions to the problem without fully hearing what is upsetting your child? We don't like to see our children suffer, so we naturally go straight to what we think will cure their suffering. While understandable, this often makes the child feel worse about their feelings.

There are also times where parents may punish their child for having big emotions. This punishment often comes in the form of verbal harm or threats, like "Stop crying or I will give you something to cry about," "You are acting like such a baby," or "Just calm down; there's no reason to get so upset." You may have heard these phrases during your own childhood, or may be guilty of using them with your child. Phrases like these ignore your child's emotions and make them feel bad for having those emotions. As a result, your child may try to hide what they are really feeling to avoid these kinds of future comments.

Effective Ways to Validate Your Child's Feelings

Validating your child's emotions requires you to find a balance between understanding that your child is upset, while also not ignoring their behaviors if they are reacting inappropriately to their emotions. It will take practice to learn how to properly validate your child's feelings. Consider the following suggestions to help you get started:

- Be present with your child. You don't have to say anything; just be near your child. When they have calmed down, let them know that you are ready to help when they need it.

- Help your child better communicate their emotions by guessing what is bothering them. For example, your older child is building a 3D puzzle at the kitchen table when their younger sibling runs up and tries to grab the puzzle, causing it to fall and break on the floor. Your child begins screaming and yelling at their sibling.

You can guess how your older child is feeling by saying, "You seem very frustrated with your sibling for knocking over your model. You were working very hard on that, and I bet you must feel disappointed now that you have to start all over." This lets your child know that you are trying to understand what they are feeling, while also modeling to them appropriate identification of their emotions.

- Validate feelings as opposed to focusing only on behaviors. Even if you do not agree with your child's emotional reaction, you can still validate your child and also find ways to praise them when they do use an effective coping mechanism to work through their big emotion.

- Normalize emotions when possible. You can say to your child that everyone feels the way they do when they are in a certain situation and it is okay to feel that way.

- Apply these principles to yourself, too. Modeling how to identify and label emotions will help your child better understand how to do the same. Always label your emotions appropriately, explain why you are feeling those emotions, and verbalize how you are going to properly handle these emotions and calm yourself down.

Now that you know how to validate feelings and behaviors, we're going to dive into encouraging those positive behaviors that you love to see.

Parental Action Plan

Make a conscious effort to validate your child daily.

Reflect on your day and identify a time when you validated your child's emotions and a time when you validated their behaviors.

10

ENCOURAGE DESIRED BEHAVIORS

Y ou've learned a lot about identifying behaviors that you don't want and behaviors that you do. But how can you implement tactics to encourage good behavior? Here, you will learn various techniques to help your child succeed at self-regulating and repeating desirable behaviors.

Responding to Behaviors

There are multiple ways you can help your child manage their behavior and encourage desirable behaviors. These strategies focus on correct behaviors and also preserve the parent-child relationship, teach children valuable skills, and improve your child's self-confidence. While you may not use every method available on a regular basis, it is important to become familiar with various techniques that you may rely on during different developmental stages of your child's life.

Praise

Giving praise has been recommended throughout this book. Praise is an effective way to highlight good behaviors because by nature, children do aim to please. The more they are praised for a certain action, the more likely they are to repeat that action. Using praise in an effective manner requires you to 'catch' your child in the moment doing something good. You want to give praise immediately after the behavior has occurred and do so in a non-disruptive manner. Remember, praise does not have to always be a verbal "great job." It can be an approving smile or pat on the back.

Imitation

Imitation works well with younger children. During playtime, you can imitate how your child is playing with their toys to show your approval of what they are doing. Imitation can also come in the form of allowing your child to show what they know. You can ask your child to 'help' you with a problem you are having. This teaches your child to ask for help when they need it and gives them the opportunity to use their problem-solving skills.

Description

Description is a way to prove to your child that you are interested in what they are doing and you are giving them your full attention. Like imitation, description works best with younger children. To effectively use description, imagine you are a sports broadcaster. You want to describe what your child is doing in as much detail as possible. This is beneficial to your child's development in a few ways. It helps younger children develop a wider vocabulary. Their self-esteem increases because they have your undivided attention. Using description when you are performing a task together can also help your child remain focused and learn to follow directions. While you are describing what your child is doing, you should also include praise when they are doing something you want to encourage.

Positive Reinforcement

Positive reinforcement can take many forms. Giving praise can be used as positive reinforcement. Rewards such as snacks, earning points towards a bigger reward, or receiving additional privileges are also common examples of positive reinforcement. Encouraging appropriate behaviors is the goal of all positive reinforcement. Reinforcement needs to be given immediately after the desired behavior occurs, which will increase the possibility that the behavior will be repeated. Parents find that utilizing various types of positive reinforcement can help encourage different behaviors.

Contracting

Contracting is a technique that can be used with older children who have a better understanding of rules, consequences, and emotional control. As with any contract, this is a written agreement where parents and child discuss behaviors that need to be addressed, find solutions for those behaviors, and establish related consequences (both good and bad). Contracts can be an effective way to reinforce house rules or your child's chores and responsibilities. The contract should include a clear timeframe when specific actions need to be completed. For example, if the goal is for your child to make their bed daily then you should establish that the bed needs to be made before they go to school. Once everything has been agreed upon, you'll also want to create a way to track your child's progress. This can be as simple as a chart that lists the task in one column and has the days of the week across the top. Each time the task is completed on time, it gets a check.

Extinction

Extinction, often referred to as planned ignoring, is when you constantly ignore a specific behavior entirely. This method is effective with many attention-seeking behaviors. For instance, a child who refuses to go to bed and cries for one of their parents to return to their bedroom is exhibiting a typical attention-seeking behavior. Each time one of the parents goes to the child's bedroom, they reinforce that behavior. To put an end to the bedtime screaming, they must ignore their child's cries and eventually the screaming will stop.

The only way this technique will be successful is if the parents consistently ignore the undesirable behaviors. Giving even the smallest bit of attention to how their child is acting will increase the intensity of the behaviors. However, be advised that with this method you must have patience. You will almost certainly see the behavior get worse when you first begin to practice extinction. Your child will become louder and more demanding as they try to get you to cave. Hold strong. The more you ignore it, the less desirable the behavior is to the child.

Remember, encouraging good behavior is just as much about giving attention to desired behaviors as it is about following through on consequences for undesirable behaviors.

Control What You Can

You cannot control your child's behaviors or reactions, but there are other factors that are within your control that can help encourage desired behaviors.

120

Environment

When we talk about a child's environment, we are referring to where they are, the objects around them, people or other children nearby, the time of day, sensory inputs such as light and sound, or the task they are be doing. There is a lot going on in your child's environment and many of these things can influence their behavior. If you struggle with behavior in a specific environment, consider what could be changed in their surroundings to positively impact behavior. Some things to consider and tips to help address environmental factors include:

- Have dedicated areas for specific activities. For instance, you can have one area dedicated to play, one area for school work, one area for sleep, and one area for calming down.

- Try to keep your child's environment as organized as possible and encourage them to clean up one item before getting out another.

- Provide plenty of mentally and physically stimulating items.

- Reduce temptation by removing undesirable objects or things that contribute to misbehavior.

- Implement small, manageable changes slowly over time.

- Monitor and limit screen time.

- Have dedicated quiet times or calming times in the middle of the day to help your child reset.

When making changes to your child's environment, it is important to keep them small instead of doing them all at once. For instance, your child may struggle to fall asleep in the evening. One change you can implement is eliminating all electronics an hour before bedtime. Allow time for this change to become 'normal' before making another change.

Set the Example

There is a major flaw in the parenting approach that tells children to do what they're told, but not what they see their parents doing. This confuses children, and since most children learn by modeling their parents' behaviors, it is hard to correct behaviors that you, as the parent, exhibit.

Leading by example does not mean you behave perfectly all the time. It does mean teaching your child how to manage their own reactions and emotions through your own behaviors. This means that when you mess up, you take responsibility, apologize, and let your child see you correcting your mistakes.

Despite what you may think, your child is intently watching everything you do. You are your child's first and most influential teacher. Everything your child has learned, they have most likely learned from you. Younger children learn from their parents by trying to please them. Older children move away from trying to please their parents to mimicking the behaviors of their parents.

You want your children to behave appropriately when it comes to managing their frustration, communicating their wants, following the rules, and listening to instructions. However, consider what else your child is learning from you.

Your daily habits are likely to become their habits as well. Diet, physical activity level, smoking, drinking, using narcotics, and personal hygiene are examples of habits that a child will learn from their parents. However, if you make your health a priority by eating a well-balanced diet, exercising regularly, and avoiding cigarettes, alcohol, and drugs, your child will learn that keeping the body in good health is important.

What about when it comes to cheating and lying? If your child sees you lie to others, they are going to learn that you don't always have to tell the truth. If you accidentally leave a store without paying for something, which can be a common unintentional oversight, what does it teach your child if you don't go back and pay for it once you realize the mistake?

Your child will also learn their work ethic from you. Many parents tell their children that to achieve anything, they will need to work hard for it. Yet some parents always cut corners, trying to find the easiest and fastest way to get things done. Others procrastinate from doing important tasks through mindless activities like watching YouTube videos and scrolling social media. These approaches do not teach a child about hard work. If you want to model a strong work ethic, you need to let your child see you working hard. Otherwise, they are unlikely to put much effort into accomplishing goals they set for themselves, getting good grades, or pushing for excellence in their life.

You can be an exemplary role model for your child by asking yourself one simple question, "If my child were doing this, what would the consequences be?" Would you be proud of them? Angry? Disappointed? If you are doing things that you would tell your child are unacceptable, then you need to consider what you should change so you can be a role model for your child.

Use Behavioral Charts

Behavioral charts are a type of positive reinforcement that lets you track your child's progress. Not all children respond well to behavior charts, especially if the chart becomes a constant reminder of how poorly they behave. However, when established properly, these charts can help promote positive behaviors. There are many ways you can create a behavior chart to help improve targeted behaviors.

To help set up your own behavior chart for your child, you can follow a few simple steps:

1. Decide what behavior you want to encourage in your child. Should they make their bed daily, clean up their toys when they are done playing, or place their dishes in the sink or dishwasher when they are done eating? The first goal you set should be easy enough to achieve that your child can earn a reward in the first week. This boosts their confidence and maintains their motivation to move on to the next behavior. Use this first behavior as a building block for other desired behaviors.

2. Choose sensible and enticing rewards. It is always a good idea to allow your child to make the final decision about their reward. Avoid monetary rewards, which often lead to inconsistencies in behavior. Instead, provide options for your child that involve the chance to do a preferred activity and allow them to make the choice. On top of these selected rewards, always offer plenty of praise for desired behaviors.

3. Now, it is time to create the chart. The type of chart you use will be dependent on your child's preferences. Some children like simple charts that allow them to put a checkmark on the days they follow through on the task they are given. Other children enjoy more colorful and engaging items, like stickers, to indicate the days they complete their task. Older children will often have a point system, where the chart keeps track of points earned that can then be used for a bigger reward. You do not have to overcomplicate this chart.

It should simply show what needs to be done and allow your child to mark when they do or do not do what is expected.

4. Once the chart is created, review it with your child. Go over what is expected, the consequences, and any rules or limitations they need to understand. Reiterate what they can earn if they follow through with the plan and how they earn their reward. Everyone in the home should be aware of the reward chart and should be on the same page about how it is being used. Once you've reviewed the directions, ask your child to help find the best place to hang the chart so that everyone in the home can see it.

5. Use the reward chart consistently. Be sure to review the chart daily with your child so that the activities listed on it become a part of their daily routine. After a week of reviewing your child's progress, it is not uncommon for parents to notice some things that may need to be adjusted to better encourage the desired behaviors. It is okay to make minor tweaks to the chart. You may need to create a chart that is more creative and engaging for your child, or you may need to adjust how they earn rewards to motivate them and help them feel more confident about making the desired changes.

One thing to keep in mind as you implement the behavior chart is to avoid having negative behaviors affect the effort your child is putting in. Do not set up rules that result in losing stickers or points, as this will only discourage them from trying. Remember, you must be consistent with your expectations. Do not give your child a day off or only implement the chart some of the time. If you want to see positive changes with your child, you need to be persistent with your efforts.

In the final chapter, we'll look at next steps moving forward and other important considerations to keep in mind as a parent.

Parental Action Plan

Choose one method of encouragement to focus on using for the next week and write it down.

At the end of the week, reflect on how you did with implementing this technique.

11

Bringing It All Together

N o parent is perfect, and you shouldn't expect yourself to be. However, you can embrace a growth mindset and actively work to learn from each and every day.

Parenting Is a Learning Process

As a parent, you will continuously be learning what works and what doesn't. You will address new situations and behaviors that will test your limits and sanity. It is okay to feel as though you are failing at times; all amazing parents experience these moments of despair. It is not easy to admit that you may have messed up in your approach or realize later there was a much better way to handle a confrontation with your child.

The moments when you feel like you are failing and messing up your child for life are uncomfortable. However, these are normal and expected parts of parenting. While it can be hard not to focus on how you have failed, it's important to maintain a continuous growth process and avoid getting sucked into a negative cycle of feeling like a constant failure.

Applying a Growth Mindset to Parenting

A growth mindset is essential for overcoming moments when you doubt your parenting abilities. Believing that you and your child are capable of making improvement is essential for lasting change and growth. When you accept that change is possible, you will find ways to help yourself and your child learn essential skills and tools to improve not just behavior, but also other areas of your lives.

If you naturally tend to have a fixed mindset, where you do not feel that change is possible, you can rewire your brain to become more open-minded. Parents who work on adopting a growth mindset will find opportunities in their perceived failures. When one thing does not work to improve your child's behaviors, you won't start feeling like nothing you do is working. Instead, you will review the method, systems, and tools you are using and consider trying another approach.

Ways to cultivate a growth mindset into your parenting style and your life in general include:

- Begin by seeing your failures as opportunities. Not everything you try is going to work, and that is okay. Avoid thinking that just because one thing doesn't work, then nothing will. When something doesn't work, use it as a way for you to learn and grow as a parent.

- Don't forget to keep your and your child's limitations in mind. Sometimes we come up with a plan that we are completely confident about, and we think our child is going to be so receptive that their behavior is going to magically improve overnight. Then you realize your child is struggling even more with this new plan and you may start to feel like you have set both of you up for failure. Remember, your child may not be developmentally ready for certain approaches to address behaviors. There may be other things you need to work on improving first, or you may be allowing other factors to dictate your expectations. Evaluate your goals and uncover what parts of the plan may not be realistic or appropriate for your child instead of labeling yourself a failure.

• Do not discredit the internal dialogue taking place in your head or the phrases you say to yourself regularly. If you are constantly telling yourself that nothing is ever going to work, then nothing will. Just because you haven't found the right thing yet does not mean that you won't ever find what works for you and your family.

Self-Evaluation and Reflection

Only when you can look at your own actions and reactions will you implement the necessary changes for the future. When it comes to your own undesirable behaviors, apply the same expectations you have for your child to yourself. Begin to get into the habit of reflecting on your own actions daily.

Self-reflection helps you identify behaviors you need to change and pushes you to find effective strategies for better managing your emotions and behaviors in common situations. Each day, evaluate how you did as a parent. What things do you think you did effectively? Did you follow through with consequences? Did you spend quality time with your child? Did you practice actively listening to your child? Don't dwell on the things you didn't do perfectly; instead, remind yourself of the things you are doing right and you will begin to see your capabilities in a new light.

When you sit down to reflect on your parenting approach, consider asking yourself some of the following questions:

- How did you help your child regulate their emotions? Did you remain calm and provide them with guidance for labeling their emotions or gently remind them of coping mechanisms to use?

- What were you consistent with? Did you follow through with consequences? Did you give out praise frequently? Did you find opportunities to show your child that you liked the way they were playing or working through a difficult task?

- How did you respect your child's boundaries, and how did they respect yours?

- In what ways were you a good role model for your child? What behaviors do you need to improve tomorrow?

- When did you clearly tell your child what you wanted them to do, as opposed to telling them what not to do?

- Review the expectations and consequences that have been outlined for your child. Are there any things that may not be age-appropriate or developmentally appropriate for your child?

- What was one thing that worked today? When did you see your child make improvements or use the skills you taught them to get through a difficult situation? Was there a conflict with your older child that was resolved peacefully? Did you negotiate and compromise with your child so that you both got what you wanted and needed?

- What did you do for self-care today? If you haven't done anything yet, what can you spend five or ten minutes doing before you go to bed?

- What method or techniques did you use today to keep your own emotions under control? Did you STOP? Did you create space between you and the conflict?

- How did you reward your child's good behaviors today? How can you do so tomorrow?

- What are some thoughts you need to let go of that are causing you to feel like a failure? Take five minutes to write down those negative thoughts and then reword them to be more positive and empowering.

- Did you spend quality time with other family members? If you are living with a partner, how did you show your appreciation to them? Did you sit down to talk and connect for at least 10 minutes?

- What are some things that you can make adjustments to tomorrow that are within your control? Remember, the environment has a major impact on our behaviors and thoughts. Is there a room you want to get better organized? Do you want to add some wall art or decor to another room to make it more inviting and warm? Find one small thing you can do that could have a positive influence on behavior and mindset.

Good Parenting Skills

It is easy to constantly think you are a bad parent, but unless you are blatantly neglecting your child, chances are that you are doing a much better job than you give yourself credit for. Every parent wants their child to be healthy, happy, and well-behaved. It is easy to feel like you are failing when one of these desires is not meeting your expectations. To help you feel reassured and to identify key parenting skills you might want to focus on more intently, review the questions below. Answer honestly to assess your parenting skills.

1. Does your child feel secure in knowing you love them?

2. Do you spend quality time with your child?

3. Do you show affection to your child daily (hugging, sitting next to one another)?

4. Do you schedule time for yourself, away from your kids, to do things that you enjoy doing?

5. Have you taken your child's developmental stage into consideration when you set expectations?

6. Do you encourage your child to do things for themselves?

7. Do you enforce discipline that is fair and appropriate for their age and what they have done wrong?

8. Have you clearly reviewed and explained the consequences for your child's behaviors to them?

9. Do you have rewards in place to encourage positive behaviors?

10. Does your child have a stimulating environment that encourages their curiosity, learning, and growth?

11. Do you or others in the home put an emphasis on education?

12. Do you support your child's interests?

13. Do you encourage your child to form positive peer relationships?

If you have answered yes to most of these questions, rest assured that you are in fact doing a great job of parenting your child. If there are questions that you could not confidently answer with a yes, you now know what things you can focus on to improve your parent-child relationship and your parenting skills.

At the end of the day, you know what's best for you and your child. Learning to trust yourself is an important step and you're already making strides towards this by choosing to educate yourself on best practices. Go ahead and congratulate yourself—it's not easy being a parent!

Parental Action Plan

For one week, at the end of each day, reflect on what went well and what didn't.

Write down the good and the bad, along with what you think the problem was and what you could have done differently.

CONCLUSION

B eing a parent is one of the most rewarding experiences of your life once you learn to successfully navigate your child's behaviors. Many parents struggle to enjoy being a parent because they spend so much time and energy disciplining, correcting, and fighting with their kids. They resort to harsh punishments and often display poor behaviors themselves to try to get their kids to act the way they expect them to. Parenting doesn't have to be a constant fight. Being a parent doesn't have to add an extraordinary amount of stress to your life because your child is struggling with self-regulation. It is possible to teach your child how to behave appropriately without losing your temper or your sanity.

This book has covered a variety of positive parenting techniques that will help you build a stronger relationship with your child. You have also learned that getting your child to behave appropriately is more about teaching them the skills they need as opposed to demanding that they stop acting out. The only way a child will learn what to do and how to control themselves is if they have parents who make the effort to guide them and model the behaviors they should exhibit.

You now have a toolbox full of tips, strategies, and exercises you can begin to implement with your child, from teaching your child how to label and express their emotions properly to handling conflict and properly asking for what they want. You have everything you need to start building the relationship of your dreams with your child: one that is full of laughter, love, and respect.

Don't spend another day pleading with or punishing your child. Instead, start today to implement the effective strategies you have learned throughout this book to encourage desired behaviors. It is possible to be a loving parent while also raising your child to be a respectful, independent, and happy human being!

I hope that you feel more confident in your parenting abilities. If you have found value in the information provided, please leave a review to share your biggest takeaways with other readers and let them know what they can expect to gain from reading this book. I believe every parent deserves to have a loving relationship with their child, and I wish you luck as you continue on your parenting journey!

We really hope you have enjoyed this book and we would love it if you could please leave a review by using the QR code below as it really helps small businesses like ours

Thank you

REFERENCES

Anderson, J. (2021, April 13). *The effect of spanking on the brain.* Harvard Graduate School of Education. https://www.gse.harvard.edu/news/uk/21/04/effect-spanking-brain

Austin, D. (2021, May 4). *6 reasons why yelling at kids doesn't actually work.* Parents. https://www.parents.com/health/healthy-happy-kids/a-parental-wake-up-call-yelling-doesnt-help/#:~:text=Yelling%20doesn

Behavioral charts: How to promote the behaviors you want. (n.d.). Hartstein Psychological Services. https://www.hartsteinpsychological.com/behavioral-charts-how-to-promote-the-behaviors-you-want

Canadian Paediatric Society. (2004). Effective discipline for children. *Paediatrics & Child Health, 9*(1), 37–50. https://doi.org/10.1093/pch/9.1.37

Changing the environment: Behavior management tool. (2019, September 5). Raising Children Network. https://raisingchildren.net.au/school-age/behaviour/behaviour-management-tips-tools/changing-environment

Coach, J. A. W. / P. (n.d.). *Myths and misconceptions about discipline.* Blog.heartmanity.com. https://blog.heartmanity.com/myths-and-misconceptions-about-discipline

Communicating well with babies and children: Tips. (2020, August 31). Raising Children Network. https://raisingchildren.net.au/toddlers/connecting-communicating/com municating/communicating-well-with-children#active-listening-with-chi ldren-tips-nav-title

Disciplining your child. (2018, June). Kidshealth.org. https://kidsheal th.org/en/parents/discipline.html

Ehmke, R. (n.d.). *Tips for communicating with your teen.* Child Mind Institute. https://childmind.org/article/tips-communicating-with-teen/

Gable, S. (2016, April). *Communicating effectively with children.* Exte nsion.missouri.edu. https://extension.missouri.edu/publications/gh6123

Gehl, M., Kinsner, K., & Parlakian, R. (2018, June 6). *Mindfulness for parents.* ZERO to THREE. https://www.zerotothree.org/resources/226 8-mindfulness-for-parents#citations

Heilmann, A., Mehay, A., Watt, R. G., Kelly, Y., Durrant, J. E., van Turnhout, J., & Gershoff, E. T. (2021). Physical punishment and child outcomes: A narrative review of prospective studies. *The Lancet, 398*(10297), 355–364. https://doi.org/10.1016/s0140-6736(21)00582-1

Herzog, E. (2020, October 2). *How parents can manage conflict with their children.* KVC Health Systems. https://www.kvc.org/blog/manage -conflict-children/

Howenstein, J., Kumar, A., Casamassimo, P. S., McTigue, D., Coury, D., & Yin, H. (2015). Correlating parenting styles with child behavior and caries. *Pediatric Dentistry, 37*(1), 59–64. https://www.ncbi.nlm.nih.gov /pmc/articles/PMC4559268/

Jaconson, R. (n.d.). *Teaching kids about boundaries.* Child Mind Insti- tute. https://childmind.org/article/teaching-kids-boundaries-empathy/

Kavan, M. G., Saxena, S. K., & Rafiq, N. (2018). General parenting strategies: Practical suggestions for common child behavior issues. *Amer-*

ican Family Physician, 97(10), 642–648. https://www.aafp.org/afp/201
8/0515/p642.html#sec-3

Lee, K. (2021, April 1). *Strategies for setting healthy boundaries for kids.*
Verywell Family. https://www.verywellfamily.com/whos-the-boss-how-t
o-set-healthy-boundaries-for-kids-3956403

Lerner, C. (n.d.). *Responsive vs. reactive parenting: It makes all the
difference.* PBS KIDS for Parents.
https://www.pbs.org/parents/thrive/responsive-vs-reactive-parenting-it
-makes-all-the-difference#:~:text=Reactive%20parenting%20is%20when
%20we

Li, P. (2022, February 23). *Reactive parenting - What it is & how to
overcome.* Parenting for Brain. https://www.parentingforbrain.com/reac
tive-parenting/

Marcin, A. (2019, August 21). *What is mindful parenting?* Healthline.
https://www.healthline.com/health/parenting/mindful-parenting

Meleen, M. (n.d.). *How to assess parenting skills.* LoveToKnow. https:/
/kids.lovetoknow.com/assess-parenting-skills

Merrill, M. (n.d.). *How to evaluate your relationship with your child.*
Mark Merrill. http://www.markmerrill.com/how-to-evaluate-your-relati
onship-with-your-child/

Mori, A. (2021, March 27). *The difference between punishment and
discipline.* Verywell Family.
https://www.verywellfamily.com/the-difference-between-punishment-an
d-discipline-1095044#:~:text=When%20it%20comes%20to%20correctin
g

Negotiating with teenagers. (n.d.). Raising Children Network. https://raisingchildren.net.au/teens/communicating-relationship
s/communicating/negotiating

*Parent-child relationship - Why it's im-
portant.* (2018, October 25). Parenting

NI. https://www.parentingni.org/blog/parent-child-relationship-why-it s-important/#:~:text=The%20Parent-Child%20Relationship%20is

Pincus, D. (n.d.). *Grandparents and parents disagreeing? 11 tips for both of you.* Empowering Parents. https://www.empoweringparents.com/arti cle/grandparents-and-parents-disagreeing-11-tips-for-both-of-you/

Pon Staff. (2021, September 28). *Dear negotiation coach: What is the secret to negotiating with kids successfully?* PON - Program on Negotiation at Harvard Law School. https://www.pon.harvard.edu/daily/win-win-daily/dear-negotia tion-coach-how-can-we-deal-more-successfully-with-our-kids-nb/

Robinson, L., Smith, M., & Segal, J. (2021, January). *Tips for building a healthy relationship.* HelpGuide.org. https://www.helpguide.org/articl es/relationships-communication/relationship-help.htm

Staff. (2 C.E.). *Parents must lead by example.* Professor's House. https ://www.professorshouse.com/parents-must-lead-by-example/

Strong families: What they are, how they work. (2017, November 24). Raising Children Network. https://raisingchildren.net.au/grown-ups/fa mily-life/routines-rituals-relationships/strong-families

Tantrums. (n.d.). Better Health Channel. https://www.betterhealth.v ic.gov.au/health/healthyliving/tantrums

Wang, M.-T. (2013, September 4). *Yelling doesn't help, may harm adolescents, Pitt-led study finds.* University of Pittsburgh News Services. https://www.news.pitt.edu/news/yelling-doesn-t-help-may-harm -adolescents-pitt-led-study-finds

What is mindful parenting? (n.d.). Headspace. https://www.headspac e.com/mindfulness/mindful-parenting

Wolf, J. (2019, June 25). *Why is reactive parenting harmful while raising kids?* YouTime Coaching. https://www.youtimecoach.com/reactive-pare nting/

ABOUT THE AUTHOR

Holly Henderson is a mother of 3 children who has been interested in parenting strategies and techniques since she welcomed her first child. She found it difficult to enforce discipline with her first child because she was so worried about creating conflict but found that this lack of boundaries actually made things more difficult. When she had her second child she reevaluated the approaches she had been using, which is when she began to learn about alternatives to traditional discipline. After finding success with these new approaches with both children, she became even more interested in studying all she could about parenting and child psychology.

Holly and her husband were raised with very different family dynamics to each other and initially had differing views on parent- ing; they didn't put too much thought into discipline when their first son was born. Learn- ing through mistakes they soon realized the importance of creating a united front and the importance of being on the same page as each other when it came to house rules & disciplines. For their own relationship & the relationship as a family; they started to create their foundations that were true to their beliefs and desires for their future together as a family.

Made in the USA
Monee, IL
27 November 2022

18679985R00085